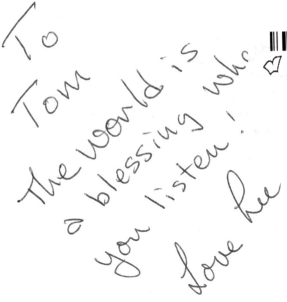

To
Tom
The world is
a blessing who
you listen!
love Lee

INTERCONNECTED ONENESS

The oak trees that abound where I live now are a constant reminder of Oneness. That is why they are chosen for this book cover. In the realization of oneness, we can always **"accept."** The trees are connected in a system of woods, sun, rain, wind, animals, ground, and sky. They symbolize that nothing exists alone, all is interdependent. The sun and the stars, as well as the ground and the worms are all part of the tree's life. I sit in its shade and wonder...*Where do I begin and end*? Certainly not just at the end of my skin any more than the tree ends in the roots or branches. They also remind me of perfection. All trees are different, and yet each is perfect and part of a perfect system. Who would be so foolish as to judge a tree and decide some to be less than perfect. Even trees which are totally changing form (dying) are perfectly providing a nurturing basis for new life.

LISTENING . . . STILL
AND ACCEPTING

How to Increase
Your Acceptance of
Perfection

by

Lee Coit

Published by:
Las Brisas Publishing
P.O. Box 500
Wildomar, CA 92595

Quotations from "A Course In Miracles" used by permission of
the publisher, Foundation for Inner Peace, Tiburon, CA

Type Set In Swiss by Ventura Publisher by
SDC-South, Laguna Hills, CA.

ISBN 0-936475-04-8

Contents

Chapter 1

We Don't Know How To Make Our Lives Work-Getting To The Bottom Of Things-Developing A Willingness To Change-Quitting Was The Place To Start-Can Getting What We Want Bring Happiness?-What Will Make Us Happy?-Looking At The Two "Me's"-Finding My Identity

Chapter 2

The First Tentative Steps Toward Happiness - Spending Time Sitting On Rocks - First Comes Willingness - Three Basic Steps-Small Insights - What Were The Laws - Waiting For The Burning Bush - The "Stiff Necked" Doubter - The Search Goes On - A Pattern Emerges - The Graduate School - The "True Love" Course - Inner Guidance Becomes Clear - My Commitment Is Most Important - Suspending Judgement In All Circumstances

Chapter 3

Traveling With An Inner Guide-Solid Direction Is Provided-My Inner Voice Becomes Very Loud-Waiting For Your Own Answer-The Total Commitment-I Enter A Strange Monastery-How Inner Guidance Worked-I Meet Two Angels-Being Guided, We Get Assistance-After "Listening,"We Can "Accept"-"Accepting" My Past, Present, And Future-There Is No Delay-God Is Not Blocked-The Wart And Pimple Theory.

Chapter 4

Chapter 5

Chapter 6

Chapter 7

"ACCEPTING" PUTS GUIDANCE INTO PRACTICE 91

"Accepting" Reveals The Power Of "Listening"-"Accepting" Changes ConflictTo Perfection-"Accepting" Lets Us "Listen" Properly-"Listening" in All Facets Of Our Lives-The Proper Use Of Action-What Mastery Is-Spiritual Mastery Takes Practice-Eliminating The Dependence On Understanding-Understanding Is Not Forgiveness-The "Accepting" Viewpoint-Releasing The Need To Know-The Bleecker Story-I Find My Teacher At Last- Finding Your Teacher-Spiritual Understanding Is Not Needed-Attack Disguised As Help-Unrequested Advice-How To Help and Teach-Proof That It's Working.

Chapter 8

"ACCEPTANCE" IS THE OPPOSITE OF CONTROL 109

"Accepting" Frees Us From The Control Prison-We Control In Many Ways-What About Control?-Four Steps That Release Control-Is Control Effective?-Standing On The Edge Of Uncertainty-This World Doesn't Work-The Chart-The Spiritual Trip-Giving and Recieving

Chapter 9

IN CONCLUSION 121

"Being" -The Three Processes are One-Oneness

GLOSSARY 123

10 Attitudes of "Accepting" (cut out reminders)

FOREWORD

This is the story of one persons's quest. As we pursue our own unique spiritual journey, we need encouragement that what we have read about the experiences of "advanced souls" can also really happen to us. When we look at such people as St. Francis, or St. John of the Cross, or Yogananda, or . . . we tend to think that they are special, a breed apart. We are in awe of them as we read the accounts of their lives. Yet each one maintained that what they accomplished, we can all accomplish.

I am not saying that Lee Coit is a saint in the classical meaning of the word. I have not seen him walk on the surface of the pool at my condo complex, nor have I seen him awaken the dead. When we built Las Brisas Retreat, I was not impressed with his space planning. In fact, I've seen him struggle with the same personal issues we all face.

Lee is just a guy trying his best to live in the world that you and I inhabit, but he is trying to live by a different set of instructions. Lee does possess a quality that all saints have. He has the courage to follow his inner guide even if he looks foolish or risks alienating those who don't understand. Lee not only "listens," but he seeks to put what he hears into action. He is not always right in what he hears or in what he does. Sometimes he does not "listen" and follows his ego, but he does what we all must do, he tries to "listen."

From one perspective, this is a "how-to" book. It gives the reader specific suggestions on "how to" make the spiritual journey smoother. From another viewpoint, this book sets forth a set of principles; principles which Lee has used and found to be Truth. Still another point of view sees this book as a series of anecdotes and short stories. Some of the material is amusing, some is sad, and some is serious, but it all emphasizes how he experiences Truth in his life.

Most of all, this book is an inspiration; a spiritual boost for us to put into action what we hear as a result of our visits to the inner silence. To be quite blunt, if Lee can do it, so can I and so can you. If this person with his human limitations can strive and with some success live his life according to God's Will, then so can you and I. Is he special? Not on your life. Is he the Christ? You bet he is and so are you and I. Read this book with your heart. Be open to your Inner Voice as you do. Each of us has a different set of learnings and if we let our own Inner Teacher show us, we will realize what they are. It is my hope that this book will encourage you to spend more time "listening to your Inner Voice" and that it will help you to become more "accepting" of the people and events in your life.

The concepts contained herein are simple. I have not, however, found them easy to put into practice. I keep trying because when I am successful, the rewards are great. The peace of God is there for all of us, right here and right now.

Dr. Eugene R. Bleecker, Ph. D.
Consulting Psychologist
Fallbrook,CA

ACKNOWLEDGMENTS

This book is dedicated to **"unsupportive"** friends, my teachers, who unknowingly forced me to examine my favorite false concepts. You have been difficult, maddening, and impossible to figure out. You have caused me to feel everything from discomfort and anger, to rage. You have been willing to teach me in a most difficult way, by **"pushing my buttons"** and not letting me avoid the Truth. Because of you, I have been able to release many of my self-imposed limitations. Until I understood about **"accepting,"** I did not appreciate your many gifts nor did I thank you for them. This book is my acknowledgment of your unique contribution of love. At the time I disliked what you did, but now I feel only love and respect for each of you.

I would also like to express my gratitude to four **"supportive"** friends, who helped produce this book; my former wife, Vikki, for her beautiful spirit and her honesty; Lois Yoakam, who insightfully served as co-editor and proof-reader; Gene Bleecker, who is a dear friend and has been a button-pushing teacher; and Roger Ridings, my trusted, long-time friend who helped develop this book's format.

INTRODUCTION

Dear Reader,

My first book, "Listening", was given to me during a single weekend. It came during two days of meditation. I simply recorded what I heard. My conscious writing of it was the adding of examples from my experiences to illustrate the main concepts. It was not something I wrote, it was a gift. For some time, I looked on it as something apart from me, as if its concepts were not my thoughts.

With the writing of this second book, the process has become clearer. I am not to write books, I am to live them. I am to share with you insights I am given by inner guidance, how I use these concepts in my life, and what happens when I do. My inner guidance is given to me for MY happiness. What I hear may not always match your beliefs or experiences and that is fine,

There is only one concept I hope you adopt. That is to always turn within to your own inner guide for your direction. Beyond that I do not know what you should do. Encouraging you to follow a specific path would violate all I believe is true. If I sound at times like I am giving instructions, it is because this is how my inner guide has instructed me. I am passing this information on in the form that I have received it.

I have defined familiar terms I use in the Glossary at the end of this book. My meaning for such terms as "God" or "Divine Source" may not be the same as yours. It would be well to check a term that is unclear or giving you concern by referring to the Glossary.

Should any of my terms bother you, please feel free to substitute your own names if they come closer to the proper meaning for you. I am sure the spiritual truths of which we speak are not affected by the limited words we use to describe them. Best of all, read with your heart and not your head.

So let's proceed. I want to share how I arrived at my present state of happiness when just a few years ago I was in the process of giving up on life.

Lee Coit
October 1991

Chapter 1

STARTING THE INNER JOURNEY

We Don't Know How To Make Our Lives Work

My goal in life until recently was to try to figure things out. My efforts to find answers were frustrated nearly all of the time. What I wanted often eluded me and, even if I got it, I was disappointed in the end. When I tried to avoid something, it followed and haunted me. Sometimes I would say to myself, philosophically, *"It will all work out for the best."* Sometimes I would pretend I didn't care. Usually I avoided this feeling of loss by searching for a new source of happiness. The truth is, I was often angry. I tried to hide my disappointment in excess pleasure, but that happiness was always short-lived. Most of the time, I simply concealed the feeling of betrayal under a mask of calm detachment. What I longed for was happiness and certainty.

In 1978, I had a chance to make a major change in my life. My partner in the advertising agency decided to buy me out. The proceeds from the sale meant I did not have to work for several years, so I decided to really enjoy myself. I vowed I would not get back in a rut again. I would live life **my way**. I thought all I needed was a fresh start.

Getting To The Bottom Of Things

I moved to California and found a house near the beach. It was my fantasy of a place to live. Recently divorced, I decided to enjoy my relationships with women

3

without making any commitments. I planned to work only if it was fun and to keep any business small and simple. After about a year of doing it **my way**, I was more unhappy and frustrated than ever before. I had become involved with a marketing business and it was a disaster. My social life was very busy, but lonely and unsatisfying. My desire to live life fully had produced two arrests for drunk driving and two nights in jail. My new lifestyle was not making me happy and I had no idea what to do next.

For the first time, I felt that life was worthless and I finally understood why someone would commit suicide. Unknowingly, I had taken the first step toward finding some real answers. I had bottomed out.

Developing A Willingness To Change

Happiness had been my obsession, yet it always avoided my grasp. I saw that as **my** failure. So I kept searching for something better. Now having used up my possibilities, I was forced to look deeper. As I looked back on my past, I saw an often repeated pattern. I had tried to find happiness following the spiritual path I was taught as a child and I had failed. I had tried to find it through success in business, but it was not there. The more **success** I found, the harder I had to work to maintain it. Success was the proverbial squirrel cage and I was the squirrel. I hoped to have a wonderful marriage and a fulfilling family life. Despite great expectations, I found failure there several times. I tried to find happiness in beautiful things, but my possessions always grew to possess me.

These failures were not only necessary, they were precisely my path to real success. Of course I did not know that then, nor could you have convinced me of that concept. I simply saw myself as a man who was not happy and didn't know what he wanted.

Quitting Was The Place To Start

In 1979, with at least half of my life ahead of me, I reached this turning point. I pondered a bleak, lonely future and wondered if my life would continue to be filled with frustration. I summoned my honesty and began to examine what I had been doing wrong. Where did I start to get off track? The search started at the beginning, in my childhood.

Can Getting What We Want Bring Happiness?

What came to mind was my first bicycle. I remembered it well. It was the first thing I ever desperately desired. It was a new purple World bike at the local hardware store. It was Christmas vacation and I was in the third grade. If I got that bicycle, I would be happy for the rest of my life. There was nothing else I wanted. It was so important, I dared not even think about it -- well, not too much. After all, our family didn't have a lot of money and the bicycle was very expensive.

Christmas morning came. There was a string tied to the Christmas tree leading out the front door. Maybe! Just maybe! I followed the string out to the front porch, then around the corner of the house and there on the other end was . . . a World Bicycle, a purple World Bicycle. My joy was unbounded. I did not care that it was not the new one at the hardware store or that it was repainted by my mother. It was beautiful! I loved it. I rode it. I washed it. I was happy to just sit and admire it. On my magic bike, I dashed around the neighborhood and explored our tiny town.

Not long after this fantastic event, a friend got a new bicycle. It was a three-speed, it was **brand-new**, and it was very fast. Slowly, over time, my bicycle became less and less special. I rode it but seldom washed it. I never just sat and admired it.

I don't remember exactly what came next. There were lots of things I wanted. I saved box tops for decoder rings and model airplanes. In high school it was making the football team and getting a letterman's sweater. Of course, as soon as possible, a car. In college, being student body president. Then my first real job, then a discharge from the army, then law school, and of course, a wife, a house, and children. Finally, my own firm with my name on the door. Then a boat, then a bigger boat, and so on. Each of these things I was sure would make me happy forever. All were things I desperately needed. I got older and the toys got bigger, yet none completely satisfied me.

I had always found temporary happiness, followed by disappointment. For a long time that was fine, I would just make new plans, find something else that would made me happy, and work like crazy to get it. **But, I never found lasting happiness with all my searching and getting.**

I have talked with many people who profess to be happy with their achievements. I always find that they believe they could be even happier if they had something else. Happier if they did not have to work, if they had more money or success, if they were enlightened, or if they had a better **whatever**. I've experienced such temporary happiness, but it was never enough to satisfy me. I wanted to be totally satisfied. Was that possible?

What Will Make Us Happy?

As I examined this discouraging past, a small thought occurred to me. I had sought these things because I had been told they would make me happy. Because others wanted them, I wanted them. BUT . . . did I really want the bike, the boat, the house, the job, the "perfect wife?" Not because someone else wanted them, but because I wanted them? I realized I did not know if I really wanted all of those things or any of them. If not, **what did I really want**? What a question!

I had gotten to the point where I knew that getting **my way** did not mean I would be happy. It was an awful revelation. It was not making wrong choices that was the problem. I could not identify what I wanted, except on a very temporary basis. Was that the reason for my failure?

For example, when I sold my business and resolved to move to California, I thought living on a large sailboat would make me happy. I had a boat designer/builder draw up plans for a 55-foot wooden ketch. In the process of selling my old 40-foot boat, extensive dry rot was discovered. The price plummeted and wooden boats, which I had loved, now seemed less practical. The final estimate to build the new boat was double the original estimate. My dream faded as I was unwilling to gamble a lot of money on something I had doubts about. I settled for a 24-foot plastic boat on a trailer which I bought from the designer/builder mostly to repay him for his time.

The story goes on. The small boat was too slow to compete in my yacht club's race program. I sold it and got a 27-foot boat that was faster. I worked hard and won a few trophies, but that was not enough. I wanted to be the best sailor in the club.

So, I bought a 34-foot boat and began to win constantly due to the boat's superior design and my crew, which included many of the area's finest sailors. I became the factory representative for these boats and considered myself quite competent since we were winning races all over Southern California. Nearly all my time was spent racing or preparing to race.

In a few years, new boat designs and radical sails were developed. Major expenditures would be required to keep my boat competitive. In the end, it was taking all my time and money to continue to win races. It became such an effort that it wasn't fun anymore.

In 1982, I retired with a lot of trophies. Sailing, which was relaxing at the beginning, had become a very difficult and demanding job. I seldom go sailing anymore, I never race, and I have given away the trophies.

My boating experience is a metaphor of my entire life. What I most want in the beginning no longer satisfies me in the end. I go in circles. What I think will make me happy is in constant flux. My mind seems always in conflict. I had made thousands of choices and they had all ended in frustration.

Looking At The Two Me's

As I examined what was happening over and over again, it seemed there were two of **me**. When one got what it wanted, the other questioned it. Inside my brain there was always a battle. It seemed the two

me's didn't agree on anything and represented two basically different concepts. One **me** was a social being with a need to be good and do the right thing. This **me** was very devoted to being a nice person despite the fact that it seldom worked. He always sought approval from others. The other **me** was a self-centered pragmatic being. He demanded results that worked for him and did not care what others thought. He was involved in a search for personal pleasure and freedom. He hated to be controlled and liked to do things his own way.

To find what I wanted, it seemed I needed clarity concerning these two **me's**. One **me** was the obvious product of what others, in the form of my parents, my teachers, my wife, my children, my business associates, and friends wanted me to be. It was very clear about what it wanted and sought it eagerly. Its desire was usually for success in some form. This was the **me** I needed to be to get love and approval from others. Love was certainly something I wanted a lot.

The other **me** seemed to come from deeper inside and represented what I wanted in my heart. Its needs were not clearly defined and were often hidden from **my** own consciousness. This **me** found its expression not so much in what it wanted, but in what it **didn't** want. It seemed very uncertain, moody, and judgmental. It often criticized the other **me** for making bad decisions and tried to get it to be more realistic. If the first **me** was the idealist, the second **me** was the critic.

Who was I? One of these two **me's** or the combination of both? Maybe I was the observer, a third

9

party, who was asking all these questions and trying to understand.

Finding My Identity

Who am I? This is a question we must all answer for ourselves. Another person's answer will not do. I now think it is not just an answer to a question; it is a lifetime experience. Sharing my experiences and my process may give you encouragement in your search, but it will not give you your answer. That you must find for yourself.

I believe the question, Who Am I? is answered only by "**inner listening**" because the **me** who is consciously asking the question does not have the capacity to REALIZE the answer. In our present minds, we experience conflict and confusion. In a world of changing concepts and identities, we never know what we truly want. It is only through "**inner listening**" that we can be guided to a higher consciousness where what I want and who I am can be known and never changes.

This book describes the process that worked for me as I sought answers to these basic questions.

Chapter 2

"LISTENING" AND "ACCEPTING"

The First Tentative Steps Toward Happiness

At the outset, I was sure of nothing. I no longer believed that God was good or that eventually everything would turn out right. The world seemed chaotic and life appeared to be a survival test with failure the certain end. I wanted some method of finding happiness and peace, here and now. Other people's elaborate explanations of life's meaning did not satisfy me. I wanted a practical method of enjoying life now or, if nothing else, the knowledge that life made no sense.

Spending Time Sitting On Rocks

I stopped nearly all business and social activity. I did not want to do anything until I had some clarity. I would run each morning to a nearby beach and sit watching the ocean . . . waiting! I spent much of this time feeling sorry for myself. Waiting for something to happen, my thoughts followed random patterns somewhat like this. If there is a God, He must use some principles or laws. If not, He is chaotic and capricious, so it's not possible to know how He works. If He's beyond my understanding, it doesn't make any difference if He exists. If He is understandable, how would one go about knowing?

Then a unique concept occurred to me. Science proves things by making an assumption and then seeking to prove the assumption is true. As long as the assumption proves valid in various experiments, it is considered true at least until it fails. We prove electricity exists by observing its effects. No one has seen electricity nor does anyone really know what it is. So let's assume there is a God and He has Principles. I could test the Principles by seeking to identify their effects and by using them to solve my problems. If they solved my problems that would prove there was a God. Since God is supposed to be loving, He might even help me. If there was no God or if He didn't help, it would be good to find that out also. I had nothing to lose by trying this experiment.

In the past, my total dedication to a goal had been the best way of attaining it. So I made a pact. I would devote one year of my life, full time, to doing whatever seemed to prove there was a God. I decided to start the experiment by running to the beach each morning, sitting on a rock, and trying to make contact. I would spend the rest of the day watching for God's effects. If after one year's effort, it was not clear He existed, then that would be it. I must say, I thought my chances of finding God, His Principles, or something sensible in this senseless world were very poor.

First Comes Willingness

Without knowing it, I had taken an important step. I was willing to give up my efforts and wait for solutions. I did this because I did not know what to do. I was to learn later that this is the first of three basic steps.

Three Basic Steps

The **first step** is you must **be still**. This is not just being quiet, but being open and alert for spiritual guidance. The other two steps came much later. I will share them now so you can see the entire process.

The **second step** is to **accept** your inner guidance regardless of how it fits your idea of what to do. That means don't try to adjust what you hear or feel in your inner being so it will match your preconceived ideas.

The **final step** is to follow that guidance by **doing** what you are guided to do. We cannot just think, we must put our guidance into action. Over and over I have been shown the importance of participation and personal experience. These seem to be three simple steps, but I can assure you this is a challenging process.

I did little else during this period but run, read, watch TV with my cat Spook, and sail. All these activities gave me a great deal of quiet time. In this state, my mind was unoccupied with worldly concerns. Meditation is a commonly accepted term for this activity. Being alone and silent was important, but getting past my concerns to a quiet mental state was the essential part.

Small Insights

I was doing what felt the most natural. I liked running because it calmed me as well as helped me lose weight. I also liked sitting on my rock by the beach watching the ocean. Often while there, little thoughts would flow into my mind. Here are two examples of what was happening during that time.

Each day I picked up the most beautiful rock I could find on the beach. When I returned home, I placed it in my yard in an old-fashioned bathtub. One day, the thought occurred to me to pick up the most common rock I could find. When I took it home and placed it among the **beautiful** rocks, I saw it was also unique. I could really appreciate its beauty. It was no longer common, but had its own special identity. I remember thinking that on a planet made of diamonds, a piece of coal would be very valuable. In this world, we use the concept of scarcity to give value to things. Maybe it should not be scarcity which gives value to things, but whether we enjoy them.

During this period in 1979, I found a great deal of plastic and garbage on the beach. I was outraged. I hated the stupidity that allowed man to continue to spoil his environment. At this time most people were concerned with atomic bombs and little was being done about pollution. What occurred to me was a most unusual thought even though now it seems quite normal. I felt that we didn't have to worry about bombs and wars destroying this planet; our real worry should be pollution. That idea filled my meditations for several weeks.

One day as I sat on my rock I had a vision of a planet in the universe far away and on it two green creatures watching the sky. They had long arms and skinny fingers which intertwined in a most loving way. Beyond their view of stars and moons, out of sight and hidden deep in the evening sky, was earth dying in its own filth. Poisoned oceans lapped on the polluted beaches. The air was yellow with acid. An orange rain fell at times and killed all it touched. Then in a flash, this toxic mess blew up in a chemical reaction. Gone was Shakespeare, Greek Mythology, all the monuments of civilization, and modern man's amazing inventions. The two creatures watched as our planet fell in a shower of sparks. Holding each other even tighter, one whispered, "Look Darling, A Falling Star, Let's Make A Wish." I felt sad, yet saw it did not matter, life would go on.

It was man who would determine if he wanted to follow the laws and survive. If the laws were violated, the outcome was inevitable. There was no punishment, only choice. What did I choose? Was I making poor choices and then expecting the laws not to operate?

What Were The Laws?

I was intrigued by these insights and experiences. They were not the **answers** I wanted, but it was enough to keep me going, especially since I had made a year's commitment. Insights were not unique in my life. None of this was beyond the capability of my own mind. I could not say I was contacting God, nor did I feel He was contacting me. To believe that I wanted something big, maybe a **burning bush** like the one in the Bible that spoke to Moses -- that would convince me. If God was contacting me, wouldn't that occurrence be spectacular and easy to recognize?

Waiting For The Burning Bush

I was reading the Bible each morning before starting my run. I would just open it and read where my eyes fell. Usually during the day something would happen related to what I had read or the thoughts I was having sitting on the beach. Little incidents on the street, maybe a TV program or something someone would say, would expand on what I had been thinking. The coincidences were very frequent and I found it fascinating. However, I am not easily convinced and these little coincidences were not enough to prove anything. I looked forward each morning to my random Bible readings with interest but skepticism. I gave them the same level of veracity as the reading of my horoscope in the newspaper. Something interesting, but? *I'll keep reading the Bible as long as it works,* I thought,*as long as the coincidences continue.*

One day I opened the Bible to a chapter where it listed all the births of people. You know, He begat Him, and Him begat Hehim, and Hehim begat Hehe, and Hehe begat Himhim, and so on for several pages. At the end, it rebuked the Jews, calling them a "*stiff-necked people.*" Yep, I thought, those old Jews were a pretty stubborn bunch.

I got dressed and started running, thinking this reading has nothing to do with me. For two weeks, the readings had been right on target.

But, this morning's reading was just a bunch of names of people long dead. That proves it, I thought, these strange happenings are just coincidences. As I ran, I realized my neck was sore from the night before. With each step, my neck got stiffer.

Stiff-Necked, that's me! If I had lived then, I would have been just like those ancient Jews. Rescued from the Egyptians, they balked at everything. They demanded constant proof. Even with a Cloud to guide them in the day and a Pillar of Fire by Night, they were afraid. Even after the parting of the Red Sea, even after being fed daily by manna, they doubted. Even Moses had his doubts. Before today, I had wondered how those ancient people could be so **stiff-necked** and not see they were constantly taken care of by God. Now I realized I was just like them.

The Stiff-Necked Doubter

I really had to laugh at myself. Talk about stiff-necked doubters! I was at the top of the list. All my life I had doubted anything I had not experienced. Even as a young child, I had put my hand into the fire to experience flames. I couldn't just take my mother's word for it. I had to feel **hot** for myself.

Then I had a most amazing reassurance. From within my mind I heard, *"Don't worry, doubters are just fine. The doubters who demand proof and will not accept a thing just because someone says it is true, are greatly loved. Blessed are the doubters, for when they are finally convinced, they never change their minds. They have eliminated all possibilities and have nowhere else to go. Just be a good doubter and doubt everything until it proves itself."* *"Yeah, I Can Do That!,"* I thought, *"Wow! That felt like contact."* The thought was certainly not one I would have created, but I really liked it.

The Search Goes On

This year of searching is hard to describe. I felt confused, lonely, and frustrated at times. Then moments later, I was fascinated by the events and thoughts that occurred. I didn't identify **then** what was happening as inner guidance, it was just random thoughts, insights, and occurrences. The idea of inner guidance came later, just prior to my first trip to Europe. At this point, the communication was spotty, unpredictable, and mostly insightful in nature.

The contact with this different thought system would happen in various ways. Bible quotes would suddenly pop into my head relating to something I was doing. I would feel strongly drawn to a special place or event.

Such an instance occurred when I was given the idea by my inner guide to buy myself a birthday present. I had received in the mail a notice that Buckminster Fuller was presenting a full-day lecture. He is the man who among other things invented the geodesic dome. The mailer was addressed to someone who had lived in my house years before, but I knew it was for me.

So on February 26, my birthday, I spent an entire day in Los Angeles with Buckminster Fuller at a workshop which he called "Integrity Day." I did not go with anyone or socialize. I really wanted to be alone and give myself a gift. That was a unique idea. I'd never done anything like that before, especially alone. I basked in the wonderful energy of "Bucky" and all he had to share. I got to meet him personally. I bought one of his books and he autographed a photo in it of him sailing.

I treasured "Bucky's" writings which gave me an expansive view of earth and its possibilities. Most especially I loved his natural concept of integrity as a principle of the universe and creation. A little later, I found Walter Starke whose books gave me an expanded concept of the "Christ." (I will describe this event in detail a little later.) These introductions happened in convoluted ways and were never planned by me. It seemed they were being orchestrated by an unseen conductor.

A Pattern Emerges

Slowly during this period, an undeniable pattern was taking place. It reminded me of a puzzle. Each incident, book, or chance meeting seemed to fit into the puzzle. I did not know what picture the puzzle represented, but I could identify when a piece fit. Books seemed to follow me home. I never picked the significant ones, they picked me. They might be on a sale table, at a rummage sale, given to me, or find me in some other way. The ones I picked consciously never seemed to really move me. During this period I would meet people, watch programs, or have other encounters that all revolved around my current theme. My part in this was just to observe what was happening and learn.

The Graduate School

After a while I remember thinking, *"This is like going to graduate school. It is as if I am being given a college course by an unseen teacher."* Each semester had a theme. Each course had a series of lessons. Lesson followed lesson. Usually I noticed the connection between the event and the current lesson only in retrospect.

The "True Love" Course

After leaving Oregon, my joy at being free from my second marriage changed to grief. I was in great pain. I felt I had lost the love of my life. I tried in vain to replace this void with numerous relationships.

At times when my ex-wife was upset, she would call late at night and talk for several hours. On a few occasions, she called while I had a female visitor. It was most difficult to hear about my ex-wife's problems with other men and then to hear my companion complain about my insensitivity to her. Finally I could stand it no longer. I asked her to please stop calling. If she really wanted to settle things between us, I would buy her an airline ticket and she could come for a visit. My current girlfriend was most upset at this prospect, but it seemed the only way to resolve things.

We set a date for the visit. After she arrived, I really enjoyed being with her and my hopes increased that we could start a new life together. We talked a great deal and had a lot of fun, but old hurts kept coming up. I couldn't understand why she was so involved with the man who I felt had caused our divorce. I could not see how she could feel love for both of us.

One night during this time, my girlfriend was so despondent over my ex-wife's visit that she got drunk. Coming home intoxicated from the neighborhood bar, she was robbed and nearly raped. At four o'clock in the morning, she called saying she needed my help. I drove to her apartment right away and tried to comfort her. I was totally confused about what to do. My girlfriend loved me; I loved my ex-wife; and my ex-wife loved me and also someone else! Should I settle for someone who loved me or try to win my ex-wife back?

On the way home, I drove along the ocean as the sun was coming up. It was an inspiring sight. I thought how lovely the world was and how many beautiful women must be in it. I would only meet a few of them in my lifetime. Many of them must be as lovable as my ex-wife. Certainly there was more than just one women for me. I felt a great sense of freedom and relief. I did not have to cling to just one person as my source for "true love." There could be numerous wonderful relationships. A feeling more than a thought came over me. I saw a world filled with millions of loving, wonderful women. Surely there was a chance for me to find love.

My desperation left me. I came into my house as my ex-wife was making breakfast. I could tell her truly, *"I love you very much, but if you don't want to be with me, I can go on without you."* It was not said in anger but in recognition of the truth. I think for the first time, I really appreciated her for who she was and not as my **only** source of love. I loved her but I could still love others. She could love others and still love me.

Later that day as we sat in my garden, she shared with me her deep feelings for this other man in her life. For the first time, I could really listen and hear what she was saying. I could see why she loved him. I could believe she loved both of us. She left the next day saying she might return. I knew as she boarded the plane that it would never happen, yet a part of me hoped it might. Two days later, she called and told me she was going to Europe with the other man. A few months later, they were married. I did not get a complete healing concerning true love or this relationship at the time, but I did feel much freer.

Learning to truly love was to take me nearly ten more years. Four years elapsed before I could write and thank them both for what had happened. I was then able to see that they had given me a great blessing and that I had not lost anything. As a result of their blessing, I was able to find love everywhere. (The end of this story is covered later in the book.)

Inner Guidance Becomes Clear

By the year's end, I knew beyond question I was being guided. I vowed to continue my search until I could hear guidance clearly in any circumstance. Now I was asking about everything -- where to go, what to do, how to do it, and mostly, what did things mean. The guidance was usually a thought, but a thought unlike my normal thoughts. It came in the form of a unique concept, a clear insight, a reminder or a remembrance. When it came to me, I had the feeling of *"yes, of course."* At times it manifested as only a slight preference or inclination, other times it was strong and could not be avoided. The solutions coming from this inner guidance were far superior to my own ideas of what to do. There was no **burning bush** yet, but I felt great and knew things would work out. It was to take longer than I imagined.

My Commitment Is Most Important

No matter how hard I tried to ask about everything, I would forget. It would be hours, sometimes a day, before I became aware I was doing it **my way** again and not asking for guidance.

Normally I would forget to ask when there seemed to be no alternative. This was very common when **good** things were happening. I always asked my inner guide by going inside if something **bad** seemed to be happening, but if something good was happening, I assumed that was the way things were supposed to be. Later when I felt anger or stress about these good things, I became aware that I had not been **"listening."** I became aware during this time that good was simply things that matched my plans. I needed to **"listen"** during these times also.

I came to see that good and bad were mostly ways I justified doing what I wanted. They were just names or terms I used to describe what was happening. These two terms were the results of my judgment, based on my experiences. What was good if I did it, would often be bad if someone else did it. What was good now, could become bad later. Good and bad or right and wrong were my own creations.They were not absolutes. They were not real!

Suspending Judgment In All Circumstances

No matter whether I thought it was good or bad, my inner voice was asking me to suspend judgment, still my busy mind, and "**listen**." It was very hard to "**listen**" when I already knew the answers. Once I broadened my commitment to ask in all circumstances, real changes began to occur. I would get directions which were very different from my ideas of how to solve the problem. I would feel in my heart that I knew what to do, yet I experienced in my mind a desire to do otherwise. It was not like doing something because it was good for me. That's an "eat your spinach" mentality which says, *Do something because it's good for you, even if you don't like it*". "**Listening**" was different; it was realizing my first choice was not the best choice for me even though my mind kept telling me it was.

This Distinction Is The Key To Discernment Between Guidance
And Personal Preference. Like Any Skill,
It Takes Practice.

Following guidance is not giving up what you want. Rather, it feels as if you are receiving a deeper perspective or a clearer insight concerning something which you thought you already knew. It is the realization that the "I" that lives in this world has one viewpoint and yet there is access to a higher or better viewpoint. It is a feeling of reaching beyond the normal and touching something of infinite truth and beauty. It is the **ah ha!** when an insight comes and you know it's right.

A simple example is when you are trying to remember something and can't. So you give up for a while, put it on the back burner, and go on about your business. Then the solution comes from deep within your being and you know it's right. It's that feeling. A feeling of knowing from beyond your own thinking that something is correct. If you know like this, you do not question any more. When you are getting inner guidance, you have this same recognition and knowing.

At this point, I could access this inner guidance, but it was not always available. Sometimes it would be strong and sometimes nothing would come. I wanted a more dependable process. I wanted it always available for all decisions and at all times. I was ready to do more, but did not know what or how. The opportunity was coming.

Chapter 3

FLOWING WITH REALITY

Traveling With An Inner Guide

By the end of my first year commitment, I was no longer in deep emotional pain and I had the feeling of somehow being on the right track. My desires and needs were simplifying and so was my lifestyle. I was using guidance, not just to get answers to my problems, but as a way to determine what to do and how to do it. However, there were still major unsolved problems in my life. I had not found a relationship that was satisfying, I lacked a sense of direction, and I was not sure what to do with the rest of my life.

Solid Direction Is Provided

From the age of thirteen, my dream had been to take a long trip to Europe. When my son was ready to leave home in 1981, at last I was free to go. I began to plan my adventure. I decided to explore Europe by car with lots of camping and plenty of unscheduled time. During this period, I had a relationship with a lovely young woman. However like all my relationships, it was an on-again, off-again affair. Just before I left, she decided to come with me to Europe. We hoped the trip would help us resolve our problems.

In preparation for leaving, we made a trip to see her parents, who lived near San Francisco. She had a history of problems with her stepfather and found him difficult at best. I decided to apply my latest experiment to this problem. I had been studying Walter Starke's book, "The Ultimate Revolution", in which he suggested that we are all potential Christs. That idea really struck me and I had been trying to be the Christ as much as possible. Whenever I was in doubt about what to do, I would ask, *"What Would The Christ Do About This?"* Then I would do what I felt the Christ would do. I was using this method of making decisions for everything.

When we arrived, her stepfather was very uncommunicative and withdrawn, as usual. I asked my guidance in each difficult confrontation with him, *"What Would The Christ Do Now?"* The effect on him of my following this guidance was remarkable. At first he was as difficult as ever, but shortly he changed and became hospitable and then downright friendly. At dinner that evening, he shared with me his great disappointment, that he was never able to pursue a career as a musician. We talked a good deal about his life. A deep feeling of compassion for this man filled me and we became fast friends. The second day of our visit, my girlfriend's mother asked what I was doing to cause such a change in her husband. I shared with her my experiences with inner guidance and the difference it was making in my life.

I took my girlfriend and her mother to Tiburon for lunch the day we left. Her mother asked me again how I was getting this information and what spiritual path I was following. These were always embarrassing questions, since I did not have a path with a name or a reliable source of information. In fact, I admitted to her I never knew what would happen next. I confessed that much of the information came from little books that seemed to **follow** me home. She asked me to pick out such a little book for her.

We found a bookstore beneath our restaurant, where I picked out a book for her. At this time, my next little book jumped off the counter by the cash register and followed me home. This book was, "Love is Letting Go of Fear" by Dr. Gerald Jampolsky. I loved it so much that when we returned to San Francisco a week later, I went back to that bookstore to buy more copies of this book to give my friends.

While there, I asked about another book mentioned in "Love is Letting Go of Fear" called "A Course in Miracles". The bookstore was out of them. Frankly I was relieved, since I did not like the title.

My Inner Voice Becomes Very Loud

While buying more of his books, I found out that the "Attitudinal Healing Center" run by Dr. Jampolsky was just behind this same bookstore. These types of coincidences were such a normal part of my life now, I hardly did more than notice them. I visited the center and discovered they gave tours and that one would start in about an hour. While waiting for the tour to start, I went out to the end of the pier and was standing quietly looking across the bay toward San Francisco when a voice behind me said, *"You've Come This Far, What Are You Afraid Of?"* Since the question seemed to be addressed to me, I turned around. Imagine my surprise to find no one there. There was no one on the pier. I was completely **alone**.

My next reaction may seem a little strange, however it is quite typical of my inability to resist a challenge. Rather than being overwhelmed at this unusual event,

I felt a little irritated. I knew what the statement meant and my reaction was, *"I'm Not Afraid. I'll Go Get That Darned Book And Show You!"* It was not until later that day that the full significance of this occurrence dawned upon me. I had found my **burning bush**.

The lady in the bookstore told me where the publisher of "A Course In Miracles" was located. Since it was only a mile away, I left to get the book, allowing plenty of time to return for the tour. As I drove to the place to look at that "A Course In Miracles" book, I made several resolutions. I would walk away if anyone tried to get me further involved. I would look at the book and if it felt ok, buy it. I would not talk with anyone, or leave my name and address, or be sold something I did not want. I expected to find a very strange place, since they were giving courses in "Miracles" and I was determined to get out of there as soon as possible.

The man who opened the door of the very normal house was dressed in tennis clothes. He was in a hurry and said, *"I'm late for my game, what do you want?"* I said that I wanted to look at the "A Course In Miracles" book. He said, *"I don't have time for that. Do you want to buy them or not?"* He handed me a big package wrapped in brown paper and said, *"There are three books and the price is $29."* I remember thinking that was a pretty good deal since I'd been paying $10 for one little book. My decision was based strictly on getting a good deal and the fact that this man did not seem to care whether I bought the books or not. The whole situation was the opposite of what I thought was going to happen. I remember thinking, they must have something if they are not anxious to sell these books.

I learned years later that this man was Robert Skutch, a well know author and a founder of the Foundation for Inner Peace, publishers of "A Course in Miracles." I am grateful for his willingness to totally be himself and thereby help me during a most critical period.

I returned to the car and opened my package. Inside I found two thick books and one thin book. Once I started reading, I did not stop for five hours. My companion drove the car back to Los Angeles, as I studied the little book called "A Manual For Teachers". After the first two pages, I knew that this was what I had been looking for. I had found my direction at last. I never got back to the Attitudinal Healing Center. I didn't need to search anymore.

Before this event, other books had been helpful, but each one contained some material with which I could not agree. "A Course in Miracles" contained only information that felt right to me. It has been well over ten years since I first started to study "A Course in Miracles" and I have never had a reason to change my mind about the pure truth contained therein.

Waiting For Your Own Answer

My point is not that you choose "A Course In Miracles" as your spiritual path. The point is:

If You Keep Looking And Asking For The Right Direction, It Will Come To You.

Even better, when it comes you will recognize it. It may be frustrating to wait, but I suggest that you do not choose what does not feel right just because you want clarity **now**. Wait until you know *"this is just for me"* and then you will study and absorb it with delight.

I still love "A Course in Miracles", but I do not study it as I did for the first seven years. In the intervening years, other books have come. Each was perfect at the time and spoke directly to me. Eileen Caddy's books were just right about three years ago. As of this writing, Joel Goldsmith is having a big impact on me. Several years ago, what Goldsmith said was nice but it did not touch me deeply. Wait . . . and what is right will come to you at the **proper** time.

The Total Commitment

I left for Europe with my new books and my "ideal" companion. I had finally been given all I needed. I resolved to use inner guidance to make every possible decision and to study "A Course in Miracles" faithfully every day. I started the Workbook which has a lesson for each day of the year. Many times the lesson's requirements involved stopping every 15 minutes to meditate. Each hour I would stop and reread the lesson. I determined that doing these lessons was my main priority. This activity was having a deep effect on my viewpoint as I traveled from place to place.

I Enter A Strange Monastery

Within 30 days, my companion left me. I'm sure she was convinced I had gone crazy. For the next six months, I was mostly alone and spent a great deal of time camping and driving around in a small car with no radio. It was the perfect "monastery" for my next growth period. I call it a "monastery" because it was the longest time in my adult life that I had ever been alone without close female companionship. Much of what I learned and what happened during that time is recounted in my first book, "Listening", published several years after my return. It was for me a time of total reliance on inner guidance in all circumstances. I had been asking for inner guidance that was totally dependable. What I did not realize was that my total commitment to the **"listening"** process was required for this dependability to occur.

During this period, my asking about everything was **vital**. I was in a strange new environment. I did not know the language or the customs. In many places I could not even identify such common things as banks, restaurants, or stores. I did not know where I was going and my old methods of solving problems usually did not work. If I forgot to ask and did what I thought was best, I eventually found myself frustrated. I did not get frustrated when I asked. Then things seemed to work smoothly even if I did not at the outset agree with the guidance. Seeing the difference between these two approaches during this intensive "test" period gave me the willingness to follow inner guidance in the following years.

How Inner Guidance Worked

A good example happened shortly after I arrived in Great Britain. Since I was in England, it seemed wise to buy a car where I spoke the language. That also proved to be only vaguely true. I wanted to spend about $900. I did not want a British car, since I would be driving mostly in Europe and thought the right-hand steering wheel would be a problem. I also wanted a convertible so I could enjoy the sun. I decided a small Citroen would be perfect and set about to find one. I made lots of phone calls and followed many leads.

I even rented a taxi for a long ride to a large Citroen wholesaler's location, spending a lot of money in a useless search. Finally I remembered to turn inside and ask. In the beginning, this was hard since it was natural to use my own judgment and I would make decisions without being aware of doing so.

One day the owner of my hotel, who knew of my fruitless quest, showed me a newspaper ad for a used Citroen. The car was located about two hours away by train and priced a little high, but I decided to go anyway and made an appointment to see it. Since I was making this long trip on the train, I decided also to go on to the beach as it was only three stops past the car's location. Leaving several hours early I took the train to the beach. There I enjoyed some fish and chips served in an English Pub along the boardwalk.

With plenty of time to spare, I returned to the station to go back three stops to meet the man with the Citroen. To my horror, the train I planned to take had been canceled. The next train would put me at my meeting a half hour late. I tried to phone the car's owner but he was gone, probably on his way to meet me at the station. Frustrated again.

I Meet Two Angels

While I waited at the station, I had a most enjoyable encounter with a widow and her retarded teenaged child. The widow told me of her wartime experiences, the loss of her husband during the war, and of her unfailing faith in God's protection. At first when she started to talk with me, I was annoyed, not wanting to be bothered. I was very concerned with my own problems. She would not leave me alone and said I looked a lot like her departed husband. She wanted to know what I was doing. I was reticent to tell her about my experiment with inner guidance, lest she think I was some kind of a radical, religious nut. I said I was just traveling. She kept asking more questions. The more I revealed about my loony experiment, the more supportive she became. As we talked, I saw her and her daughter as God's messengers. She was very encouraging and told me of her deep faith in being cared for by God. She had no apparent reason to be so grateful, having been widowed during the war and left with a daughter who required total care. I don't now remember all that was said, but I still remember that meeting with fondness and love. Since that encounter, I have met many of God's loving angels. Now I recognize them more quickly.

By the time I got to my stop, the car and its owner were gone. I was discouraged and disappointed, but I remembered that woman and her daughter and their love and faith in God's protection. *"Don't Worry,"* I heard *"All Is Fine."*

I walked across the street and looked in the window of a car agency. I was just passing time until the next train arrived. The dealership was closed, but as I turned to leave, a man came to the front door and unlocked it. I asked him if I could look at his cars. When I told him what I had to spend, he said he had nothing in that price range. We talked about leasing a car, but he said he didn't do that. Then he said, *"You know, I do have a trade-in on a new car you could buy for that price, but it's a Skoda."* I had never heard of a Skoda. He took me behind the building where it was parked and I remember thinking that it was cute in an ugly sort of way.

He had sold the car new when he was working at another dealership. He said he knew the owner quite well -- it was a little old lady. Where have I heard that before? He assured me that the car was in excellent condition. It looked well maintained and had low mileage. The problem was that few people wanted Skodas. They are very basic and simple cars. It did not match my picture in any way, except for the price. It was not a convertible, it was English drive, and it was plain and slow. However, it felt right. The man put new tires on it, gave it a lube and oil change, and washed it. The total cost was less than I had budgeted. I picked up the car two days later.

Being Guided, We Get Assistance

Without going into great detail, I must report it was the perfect car for me. First being slow, it forced me to take back roads and not to hurry. This gave me many opportunities to stop and do my hourly lessons and also to practice "**listening**," though I had no name for this process at that time.

Being an English drive it announced that I was a foreigner in every European country, which turned out to be a real advantage. People love to help strangers and I got many invitations to stay in homes and be shown around the local area. Being simple, it was easy to repair by anyone who could fix a lawnmower. It also got fantastic mileage, allowing me to go anywhere I wanted on my limited budget. It never left me stranded and was very dependable in an erratic way. My experience of this "listening" process has continued to expand over the many years since this trip.

After "Listening," We Can "Accept"

Roughly five years ago I became aware that a new dimension of **"listening,"** that I call **"accepting,"** was happening in my life. It became evident with the founding of Las Brisas Retreat Center and the publication of my first book. My conscious asking about everything was no longer critical. However, I must emphasize that my desire to be guided was always present. Now, step-by-step, I was in a literal sense being guided along a definite path. I did not have to ask what to do. What was needed was done. What was not done was not needed.

"Accepting" was not a level I sought. It was simply a natural progression in which I experienced that before I could ask, what I needed was provided. More and more it became unnecessary to ask a specific question. My life was naturally unfolding on its own. It was not important for me to understand the next step in that unfoldment, but only to enjoy it and allow it to happen. My job was to not interfere.

"Accepting" My Past, Present, And Future

I became aware of this flowing nature in my whole life, past as well as present. Past events that seemed to be unrelated detours now fit into an integrated whole. I still remember my surprise when this was revealed for the first time. Each person and event fit together as part of a beautiful plan, despite what I had experienced at the time. My former disjointed, roller-coaster life now was re-seen as a wonderful unfoldment. I think my first real breakthrough regarding this was seeing that my ex- wife and her new husband had been perfect in helping me learn about love. Any semblance of anger faded and I became most grateful for their actions, which at the time had caused me great pain, but now appeared as a wonderful gift.

I was told that, despite my beliefs, I had never hurt anyone nor had anyone ever hurt me. Everything and everyone were necessary for my awakening. Others joined me to also awaken, though at the time it might have seemed otherwise. At this point, a wonderful new concept was given me, though I spent several weeks struggling over it. I was to learn that there was no such thing as **blockage**.

There Is No Delay

In 1985, I went to Russia and then back to Europe to give some lectures and workshops. "**Listening**" had just been published in its present form and I loved having the opportunity to share it with everyone, even a few Russians. During that trip, I met many people in Europe who wanted to know more about "A Course in Miracles" (ACIM). I had lots of ideas about how this could be done based on my experience in marketing. My love of "ACIM" was unbounded and I was looking for some way to express it. Helping promote "ACIM" in Europe seemed the ideal project. I was very concerned about some of the confused representations of this material that seemed to be taking place there.

I took my ideas to the Foundation for Inner Peace, the non- profit organization that publishes "ACIM". They are a group of people I respect and admire greatly. In fact, at the time, I looked to them as examples of what I hoped to be. I explained my ideas to some members of the group and they were very interested.

Things seemed to be falling into place in a wonderful way and I was sure that my inner guidance was right on target and that I was doing exactly what I was supposed to do. That is, until one person in the group, who arrived the next day, resisted my ideas. I had always seen that person as very spiritual and devoted, so I was shocked when the resistance seemed to come from fear and limitation. How could such a person allow himself to sink to those levels and oppose my wonderful plan? I left hurt and resentful, seeing myself **blocked** by a person who could not get past his ego, despite being a spiritual teacher. My resentment became a fever and a sore throat. I could hardly speak.

This was a real problem as I was scheduled to be one of the main speakers at a week-long conference starting in two days. I had committed to give several lectures and workshops during this period and now found it difficult to even talk.

I struggled with my disappointment, my sore throat, and my view of being blocked by someone's ego. The first day of the conference, I was barely able to finish my workshops. I shared my discomfort with a co-lecturer, Carlagaye Olsen, a wonderful, bright, and funny lady. I told her of my disappointment at being blocked by a fearful, limited viewpoint, especially since it was expressed by someone who should know better.

She shared a similar experience in her life and how she, too, had felt blocked and disappointed because of another's resistance. He, like my "opponent," was someone whom she had looked up to. She also shared the lesson she had learned from that experience. She came to see that, even though the event seemed very negative at the time, it was a huge **blessing**. It had given her a push in the right direction. Had she followed the path she preferred, it would have meant continued dependence on another's approval. That would not have left her free to follow guidance from her spiritual source, since she would have been looking to this other person for guidance in what to do. She said, *"Even people we see as blocking us, regardless of their motives, can only bless us."* She reaffirmed that God is not frustrated or blocked by anything. There is nothing happening but God's direction and guidance, no matter what seems to be happening.

God Is Not Blocked

Of course that was true. It was a breakthrough for me. My sore throat lasted only a short time. My inner guide, always eager to make light of seemingly serious situations asked me, *"Are things still sticking in your craw."* No! No! I was free. There was no such thing as **blockage** from any source. Before, I had believed that people had to follow guidance and be loving to help me. Or at least I had believed the reverse, that I could be **blocked** by the ego and must avoid or fight against it. That was not true! Nothing could block God's plan for me or even slow it. It did not matter what others' motives were. It did not matter whether their actions were based on love or fear. *"God's Will Was Being Done, Always."* It is being done here and now, because it is the only real power.

Following guidance, we are unopposed, all appearances to the contrary. We only need to **"accept"** what is happening and ask to see the blessing, for it is always there.

My loving spiritual brother, who did not agree with me, was right. His refusal to support my plan was truly divine direction. Not because my plan was wrong or right; it went much deeper than that. I was free to continue with my plan if I desired. What I wanted was permission and, beyond that, authorization. I learned a great lesson. I did not have to be authorized. My authority and my support come from only one source . . . God. What a blessing my wonderful "opponent" had given me. If I had been successful in getting the group's permission, I would have looked to that group as my source for direction. My job was to look to my inner voice for direction, regardless of whether others did or did not approve.

It does not matter whether, from our perception, someone is coming from fear or motivated by deepest love. Their actions always result in loving benefits for us. Our happiness comes when we are willing to see the wonderful gift that is always offered. So the direction was not to go to Europe to live and work, but to stay here. My authority to lecture, write books, give workshops, play golf, drink wine, or do whatever, comes from only one source . . . **God.**

The Wart-and-Pimple Theory

From this wonderful experience grew my Wart-and-Pimple Theory. Everyone comes to bless us with love and beauty or with warts and pimples. It is easy to accept guidance if it appears as love and beauty, but inner **"listening"** and **"accepting"** will also reveal the love and beauty when what we see is warts and pimples. Now we really begin to understand and apply the concept of **"accepting."** Every person can only give us love, but we can choose to see it otherwise. Being open and **"accepting"** all gifts in whatever form allows us the vision to see what is truly happening, both at a material and spiritual level.

Knowing this, it is easy to trust what is happening and to **"accept"** it. We know it is supposed to be happening. We are the only ones who can decide our experiences. We choose the feelings and we create the effects we experience by our thinking. When we **"listen"** and first turn inside, we often ask for people, things, and events to change. We ask for different experiences, ones that fit our pictures.

As we grow in trust and awareness by following inner guidance, we come to the point of **"accepting"** all that is happening. We begin to look for the blessing in each event and person. Nothing truly comes to us but good, but we have a very limited idea of what is good. How do we get beyond this limited viewpoint? How do we use vision to see what is really happening? Let's examine that issue next.

Chapter 4

DON'T ASK FOR THINGS, ASK FOR VISION.

Seeing Beyond Forms To The Reality

In 1985, I was guided to leave the Retreat Center where I had been living and directing the building program. Invitations came for me to lecture in many places both here and abroad. The income from the sale of the book, the workshop fees and my rentals allowed me, at last, to totally end my ties with the advertising business.

For the next two years, I devoted my time to traveling, lecturing, and a new relationship. I moved to the San Francisco area and rented out my home in Laguna Beach. The Retreat Center was being run by a nonprofit foundation. The eight founders, including myself, who had taken out loans to build the center, hoped it would soon be able to sustain itself and eventually be owned by the Foundation. The founders planned to give the money they were paying on the loans as a contribution to the Foundation when it became viable.

Its Easy When It Matches Our Pictures

Many people worked on the Las Brisas project and numerous methods were explored, yet the Retreat was not able to sustain itself. On weekends often large groups would come up to help with a project and enjoy the facility. However, when the Retreat was finished and began to charge for its use, many of these visitors did not return. The founders were required to financially support the Retreat to a greater degree, at a time when we had hoped our support would be unnecessary. There seemed no end to the need for our financial involvement and no way to change the situation within our group. It became evident that new funding and new ownership needed to be found.

We all hoped the Retreat Center would continue in some manner, but we seemed unable to find a solution which we could all support. Each of the partners had invested about $10,000 in the project as of late 1987. Wanting to be free of the Retreat, I resigned from the board and offered to sell my share for $1 to anyone who would take on my part of the financial commitment.

I also offered to take on the responsibility of the Retreat if my partners would give me their shares for $1 each. I did not seriously consider what that would entail. The offer came from a deep feeling of wanting to be fair and hoping that the Retreat would be given a chance to be a reality.

Time May Be Needed For A Healing

Months went by and there were many meetings, much discussion, heated arguments, and beautiful personal healings, but no resolution. I could see that the development of Las Brisas was very different from other projects with which I had been involved. I was learning patience and tolerance. In the past I had pushed hard to get the outcome I wanted. Now I was being directed to wait, be patient, and watch.

I embarked on a lecture trip to the Midwest and the Southwest, realizing I would be faced with finding a place to live on my return, since my girlfriend had sold her home in San Francisco where we had been living. Upon my return from the lecture trip several months later, nothing had been resolved about the sale and having no place to live, I moved into the Retreat which was still unfinished and nearly empty at that time.

Partial Vision Is All I Need

In guidance, I was told to help anyone who wanted to buy the Retreat and that, if I was to own and run it, it would be given to me. So for the next month, I lived at the Retreat and assisted all the people who came, as the partners tried to find some way to solve the problem.

In the end, no one bought it. My partners, one by one, came to me and asked me to take over the project. As each obstacle to my ownership appeared, it melted away. On January I, 1988 Las Brisas Retreat with all its potential and all its obligations and debts, had been turned over to me.

Walking The Tightrope Without A Net

I had no idea what would happen next. I was told the night I was given the Retreat, *"Now If You Are Willing, You Will Go Forward Without A Safety Net."* I knew what that meant. I had been willing to follow inner guidance because it brought wonderful results to my life. However, during the first nine years of following guidance, I had always maintained a safety net through my advertising business and my rental property. Since all my assets would have to be sold to support the Retreat, the safety net would have to go.

Vision Sees NOW Clearly

This would put my guidance to the full test with no holding back. I would have to rely totally on God for supply in all things. All my assets would be used. There was no other assurance, no help from the outside.

I would have to totally trust in my Source. I had asked for vision in the past to see into the future and discern what would happen. I wanted this so I could do a better job of controlling things. Now I was to give up control and even the **hope** of control. I was to use vision to recognize that my supply came moment by moment from God as manifested though various people and things. Vision only sees Reality which is the present. There is no future other than NOW. Vision, as we experience it in this world, is clarity about what is happening, it is not another reality.

I Remember Solomon

Demonstration of vision was to be the next step in my process. Thinking about the overwhelming project before me, I remembered the story of Solomon, the king of Israel who succeeded David. Before becoming king, Solomon had reservations about his ability. Compared to David, the great king, who had united Israel, who was he? Could he do the job? Not relying on his own ability and judgment, he turned to God and prayed for an understanding heart to judge God's people and be their king.

Once, he had to decide which of two women, both of whom claimed to be the mother of the same baby, was its true mother. Instead of trying to figure out the real mother from the testimony or appearances, he used a visionary approach. He offered to cut the baby in two and give each woman an equal half. The real mother, whose love prevailed over her desire to be right, quickly gave up her demand for the child. The wise king, seeing this demonstration of love, determined the true mother and awarded her the child.

How Do We Use Vision?

Now I had to turn to my Source on a daily, hourly basis. If ever someone needed vision, it was me. I had neither the strength, knowledge, or assets to operate the Retreat for an extended period. While this was evident from the beginning, it became even clearer as I went along. Questions and fears flooded my mind. I had no idea of what to do **now** that I was totally committed. I remembered only what I had heard from the beginning, *"I Will Provide All That You Need."* I hoped so.

The Road To Vision

Let me give you a small example. The road to the Retreat, in the beginning, was very bad for nearly five miles. Shortly after I came to the Retreat, most of the road was improved by our local road district. There was, however, nearly one mile left that never got fixed and was made worse by the water company putting in a huge tank nearby. I could not afford to fix it myself and heard from my inner guide to do nothing.

The water company began to install water lines in our area and that made the road even worse. I wrote to the Water Company on several occasions and visited once to see if they would fix it. Finally they agreed to do something when the construction was finished.

Time dragged on for nearly a year and I was getting very upset. People who visited the Retreat complained about the road. The water company seemed to have forgotten about their promise, yet my guidance was to do nothing about it.

The eventual outcome was that the water company not only improved the road as far as the entry to the Retreat, but they oiled a large section of it. It was more than they had promised and far beyond anything I would have asked them to do. I feel that my harassment of them would not have accomplished this result. Yet, you will never know how many times I wanted to go to the water company and raise hell. I would always meditate first and hear, *"Be Patient, All Is Well."* It was a wonderful lesson in **"accepting"** and letting God do the work in the proper time. These situations seem easy as we look back knowing the final outcome, but at the time they require courage and trust.

Do We Give Up Logic To Have Vision?

Many people believe that to have vision, they need to suspend logic and reason. I do not concur. There is nothing wrong with logic and reason. They are also attributes of God, who is reasonable and logical. We can use logic and reason to assemble facts for a proper outcome. If our facts are right, the answer will be right. But if we don't have all the facts or our facts are false, reason and logic will evaluate falsely. At our current level of awareness, it is important to realize we almost never have all the **facts**.

Vision Occurs Naturally

By using vision, we connect with the One Mind which does have all the facts and sees clearly past the false evidence. **"Listening"** by going within is our only access to Truth. Our connection with vision is never broken, but it can be ignored. It's like putting your hand over your eyes and blotting out the sun. It does not change the sun but only your awareness of it. Vision occurs naturally when we suspend our judgment. That is, we see the sun when we take our hands away from our eyes. In a spiritual sense, we are the only ones who can remove our hands from our eyes. God will not force us to see. That would violate our free will, which is one of His exceptional gifts. "**Accepting**" helps us to suspend judgment and creates the condition under which vision occurs without effort on our part. It is the act of taking our hands from our eyes.

Faith And Vision Go Together

We often think that we need to have faith if we do not have vision. That is not true either. Faith and vision go together and are of the same substance. I was very aware when I moved to the Retreat that I might become **stuck** in that situation. On the other hand, I hated to see the project be abandoned. My personal judgment saw the many problems I would face and the difficulty of turning the Retreat around. Being in a comfortable place, I could see little benefit in placing myself in such jeopardy. I thought I needed to suspend my logical judgment and be willing, despite my better judgment, to make a "leap of faith."

That was not the truth. I did not have better judgment, I just did not have all the **facts**. I did not see the many gifts and blessings that would flow from being willing, without any good evidence, to go forward as directed. It was not a "leap of faith," it was a willingness to continue to take each step as it unfolded, regardless of my own **logical** judgment.

The Retreat has been the most challenging situation I have ever experienced. I have ended my lifelong struggle with dependent relationships as a result of being at the Retreat. I have also given up the need to be a rescuer, a compulsive helper, and a "nice" guy, which is part of the same healing.

My Relationship Search Ends

When I moved to the retreat, I thought I would be alone for a long time. Within six months, Vikki joined me and for five years we had a beautiful relationship. That painful divorce has become a huge **"blessing"** in terms of my spiritual growth. By **"accepting"** it I can see my pain was caused by my expectations and my plans. I have learned I am never alone and I need not search for companionship and love. By **"accepting"** everyone just as they are and not demanding they follow our plans, we can be at peace and experience love.

Our Part In The Guidance Process

We are not pawns in some grand scheme. We are vital partners. To do our part, we need to recognize honestly that we do not understand most situations. We need to be aware that our fear and our limited viewpoints are causing us to make poor judgments. Our part is to be willing to move past these fears and their false solutions, to open our minds and to **accept** vision. I experience this vision, not as a solution to a problem, but rather seeing things from a different perspective. I have the sense of seeing with new eyes so that what was a problem before is one no more. My experiences while running the Retreat were never what I feared. All that I needed was sent to me whether it was a source for roof tile, a telephone system that worked, an insurance policy, a reliable power plant, or the ideal partner. Always the right people showed up when needed and when they left, others came to take their place. We always had enough money to pay our bills. Just enough with no extra. If we had a busy month, we had lots of bills. If we had a slow month, we had few bills. The only effort on my part occurred when I worried about how it would all work out, did not "**listen**," and tried to do things on my own. All that happened then was that I wasted time and became unnecessarily fearful.

Step-By-Step

I often ask people who report difficulty in "**listening**" to inner guidance if they know what to do **next** -- not how to solve the problem, but simply what feels right to do next, right now. If they hesitate, I suggest, *"Do you know something you could do right now about that?"* In most cases, they say, *"Yes, I know."* That is all we have to know, the **next step**. What we want to know is, *"How will it all turn out?"* We desire to know more than one step because we seek to get back into control. You cannot be in control if you take one step at a time. This concept is essential to receiving guidance.

Give Us Our Daily Bread

We seek God as if the all-powerful, all-loving, and all-knowing could possibly lose us or we could really lose Him. We ask, *"What Is God's Will For Us?"* Do we believe God doesn't constantly show us? Is He incapable of communicating His Love to His creation? Mostly our supplications come from lack of trust and a desire to have things another way. They are not really prayers, they are **complaints**. They are the voicing of

49

our fears. They are requests for stockpiles of things so we won't have to worry about running out. These requests may even include a desire for a stockpile of love, companionship, health, and understanding.

I was asked once by my inner guide, when I was feeling a need to stockpile, why I wanted to get a lot of stuff. He said, *"If you had the richest father in the world and he gave you all you needed before you asked, and if he paid all your bills as you incurred them, would you want to carry around a lot of money and credit cards?"* I had to admit it would be unnecessary. All that we need is supplied on a daily basis. This is our **daily bread.** The Lord's Prayer is not for a lifetime's, a year's, a month's, or a week's supply, but "To Give Us Our Daily Bread." Daily bread is living NOW and following guidance step-by-step. It is doing today what you are guided to do, and have the energy and wherewithal to do. Energy and wherewithal are part of guidance.

Is This A Mind Control Technique?

Vision attained through **"accepting"** is very different from affirmations, positive thinking, visualization, or other forms of mind control. These methods work because the human mind is very powerful, not of itself, but because our faith is placed in it. Faith in vision is faith in Truth. Positive thinking and other methods of mind control reach no higher than the **mind** of the thinker. This human mind will always be limited because it is not God's Mind, which is our **real** mind. Positive thinking seems better than negative thinking because it brings what we call positive results. Positive results match our pictures of reality so we like them, but that does not make them Reality.

The Limitation Of Positive Thinking

Affirmations, positive thinking, visualization, neuro-linguistic programming, (NLP), fire-walking and other mind control systems work to bring us things and demonstrate the power of faith to change our experiences. They are all ways of using our human mind to control our experiences. They bring about events which are more in line with what we think should be happening. As you can see, they all rely on our ability to use our human minds to control. They do not get us beyond our limited thinking as humans. They are not bad methods, but they are **limited** methods.

Vision is the step beyond the human mind. It is a view of the material world through spiritual eyes which is unlimited. Whatever we seek to create with our human minds will be limited because the source is limited. The "creations" of the human mind remain in the material realm and will always disappoint us in the end. Since we are in Reality, unlimited beings, nothing limited will ever satisfy us.

"Accepting" Is Demonstrated By Action

Where do we daily place our faith? That answer will show us what we really believe. We may desire vision and declare our faith in God, but if we continue to make elaborate plans for our protection and believe ourselves vulnerable, what do we believe? If we defend ourselves from others yet desire love and forgiveness, what is our belief? Do we have faith in God or our insurance policy? Do we have faith in God or our personal wisdom and strength? Which do we use in time of stress? If our decisions are governed by fear of any kind including fear of an inadequate supply, we are not putting our faith in God.

All the plans we make and all the concepts we hold interfere with our experience of Reality because they are based on a belief in our own human ability. Faith and belief in other powers besides God is not bad. They just will not bring the desired results. If we need to make plans to reduce our fears, we should recognize them as temporary measures, only needed until our faith is more soundly placed. Plans are always **limitations** we are placing upon ourselves. We should never make gods of them. We should be willing to change them or let them go.

The Green Monsters

Several years ago, I was lecturing in Amsterdam. At the end of the first day, I suggested that the participants turn over their dreams that night to inner guidance. The next day the lady sitting next to me, who had been silent the day before, could not wait to share her story. She said she was a spiritual healer and, for more than a month, had been plagued with a horrible vision. Each time she looked out of the corner of her eye she saw an ugly green being. It was not only fearsome but seemed to be growing larger each day.

She had been afraid to speak to anyone about it, fearing they would judge her to be a poor healer. She had tried everything to get rid of it and nothing had worked. Last night, she reported, the monster came to her in a dream and stood directly in front of her.

It was so large she could not avoid looking at it. She became fascinated by its beautiful blue eyes. Instead of looking away, she decided to talk with it and asked its name. The monster replied *"Jealousy."*

She asked why it was following her and the monster said, *"I have something to tell you."* The lady told the monster she was willing to listen and the monster began to talk about her relationship with her ex-husband. She said that during the talk, she learned a great deal and many things that were hidden in her feelings came to the surface. When she awoke in the morning, she felt a great relief from this dream meeting. Looking over to her right, she still saw the green monster but it was much smaller. She reported a deep gratitude for its help and knew that it would soon be going away.

We all loved her experience and her willingness to speak with her monster. I suspect we all have green monsters of which we are terrified. I know they come to bless us, if we will only face them and hear what they have to say.

Can We "Accept" Perfection?

Vision sees everything, including us, as perfect. **"Accepting"** we are perfect and looking out from that perspective, we see everything we encounter as perfect. Being perfect, it is not our job to attain perfection. In our present state, we are like a person who is six feet tall and thinks he is five feet tall. He finds himself hitting his head a lot and not able to find clothes that fit. So he prays not to hit his head anymore and to be led to find the right clothes.

The answer he hears as he prays is, *"You Are Taller Than You Think. If You Release The Idea That You Are Five Feet Tall, Your Problems Will Be Solved."*

We cannot change what **really** is, nor can we change who we really are. Change would deny that God's creation is perfect. We must place our perfection in the Hands that created it and allow Him to restore our awareness of our perfection to us. Our job is not to judge His efforts to guide us because we don't like the form it comes in. One of the ways we reject the awareness of our perfection is to believe that we can learn, improve, and come to know what perfection would look like. We don't understand perfection.

Seeking to improve your spiritual, perfect self is the same as thinking you are five feet tall and practicing to be six feet. It just doesn't work. You are already six feet tall, your practice is wasted. You cannot become something you already are. We must drop our "small" concepts and be willing to **"accept"** all circumstances, pleasant in our eyes or not. Then we create the conditions in which vision allows us to see clearly. Hitting your head constantly is a sign you are much taller than you think. **"Accepting"** these bumps and asking for clarity lets you recognize your perfect reality. Perfection is **not** a standard against which all things are measured and judged. It is impossible to judge Reality since there is no outside standard that can be used as a measurement.

Honesty Is Vital

What is needed most is honesty about what we feel. The willingness to express how we feel, what we really think, and what we really want is essential. Too often people feel it is wrong to feel angry, upset, needy, or concerned. Honesty takes the form of a willingness to look at our **monsters** and talk with them. Our inner guide can dispel only the illusions we are willing to bring to the light and not hide. They are usually not pretty sights in our eyes. The desire to hide our "unlovable" parts is difficult to avoid. We all long to get approval. We greatly fear risking its loss. Yet I can report on every occasion when I have been willing to be open and vulnerable and face my **monsters**, a healing has occurred. Being open, I feared rejection, but found understanding and love all around me.

Children Can Show The Way

We can learn much from children who, in their openness and willingness to express exactly how they feel, find love and friendship everywhere. We are able to be open and vulnerable with our friends and that is why we love them and they love us. We can extend this to everyone and make everyone our friend.

What would that look like? Telling everyone who bothers you that you hate them? Being a bore by revealing every single thought as it occurs? Certainly not. It is just to honestly express your feelings, **"listen"** to your **monsters**,and take responsibility for your perceptions as they are. I believe it's fine not to love everyone at this point in my awareness. I am sure no good comes from faking it. I am only asked to be willing to honor and **"accept"** everyone as they are.

Honesty Is Not Blaming

Honesty is not telling another about their faults with a desire to have them change. It is taking responsibility for how you feel about what they are doing. There is a **big** difference. One viewpoint seeks to make another wrong. It believes that if only they would change, you could be happy. The other attitude takes responsibility for what you think and how it makes you feel. It does not find the other **wrong** but acknowledges the monster within you and seeks to talk with it.

I believe everyone is doing the best they can. In fact, one of the great causes of false perception is that we think others should do what we think is right. It takes courage and honesty to give up these perceptions and simply **"accept"** what is. Let's look more into how perception works and can bless us.

Chapter 5

PROPER USE OF WILL AND RESPONSIBILITY

Doing Our Part In The Inner Guidance Process

As long as we believe our thinking is not the sole cause of our problems, we will look outside ourselves for solutions. While we believe problems come from somewhere else, we will waste time analyzing and seeking solutions at the level of the problem's manifestation, instead of looking within our own thinking where both cause and solution are contained. Not realizing our cherished beliefs and false concepts are the source of our problems, the **only cause** goes undetected. Until we seek within our own mind, the solution of our problems will escape us.

Our Beliefs Are Responsible For Our Experience

We must understand and accept this truth if inner guidance is to become meaningful. We need to look at all aspects of this principle because it is central to seeing clearly what is happening in our lives. We may even intellectually accept this concept as true. Yet as difficult situations occur, it is very hard to recognize that our beliefs cause these problems. It seems evident that our problems are being caused by others.

It is important to realize when we **"accept"** the situation or person, that the situation or person probably will **not** change. My experience has been that no change usually occurs except in my viewpoint. A change in the other person or in the actual event is not the measurement of success. What changes is how I experience the other person, the situation, or the event.

The Choice You Always Have Is How You Will Experience The Event. You Can Always Change Your Mind And Experience Peace And Reality.

We begin the process by recognizing that the experience of something happening to us is the product of our own beliefs. It may be hard to accept this, but when we make a different decision, we will see that our experience always changes. If we don't do this -- accept that our thinking is the cause of our own problems -- we remain stuck. Until we look within, we will always be victims despite all attempts to free or defend ourselves. **We are the only ones who can free ourselves.** We will discuss three steps that can be used in this releasing process shortly. First let's examine how we fool ourselves.

Projection Makes Us Blind

How do we fool ourselves that we are not the cause of our problems? We do this by projecting the cause onto someone or something else. We say, *"I would be happy if only_____ (you fill in the blank) was not happening to me."* How do we recognize we are projecting? Very simply, we learn to recognize the **signals** of projection. These signals are always helpful and need to be recognized even if they are not pleasant. Our concepts cannot be corrected unless we acknowledge these signals or upsets when they occur.

Signals

Whenever we feel stress, mental fatigue, distress, anger, fear, blockage, annoyance, or a desire to distance ourselves from someone or something, we are getting **signals**. In short, if you are not happy, you are getting a signal. These wonderful signals cannot long be ignored or hidden. If you try to avoid them they will get louder. How terrific!

If we try to say the signal is caused by someone else, it will not work. That is what we do when we project. We say this anger is not my signal, you caused it. It's for you. We are angry with the projected cause, the other person, and hope to feel better. However, the signal, upset will not go away, no matter how much we try to get rid of it by projection. We still feel upset, despite our belief that another is responsible. If projection worked, wouldn't we feel better? So don't fool yourself. **"Listen"** to the signal's message, find out what it is saying and what false belief is causing it.

Answering Our Phone Calls

Whenever we are unhappy, upset, or angry we are getting a phone call from our spiritual source. No matter what it feels like, we should never ignore it. These spiritual phone calls must be answered because the phone will keep ringing until we do. There is no way to disconnect our spiritual phone. We will eventually answer it and then we will get real help.

How do we answer? We look at the cause of our signal. We look at our concepts of the situation. The cause of our upset, no matter if it be slight or violent or any feeling in between, is always something we believe about ourselves which is not true. A better description is that it is always a limitation we are putting on ourselves which is not real.

My problem with relationships was based on just such a limited thought which I held about myself. The recurring problem was that I would find someone who made me feel very happy for a time, but always after a while the relationship became too difficult to continue. I had numerous unhappy relationships, despite a compelling desire to find my one true love.

The "True Love" Struggle

I had gone to Europe with a companion, as I mentioned. I hoped for the umpteenth time that this would be the "girl of my dreams." After thirty days of getting more and more restless, she decided to return to the States. I was trusting my inner guidance at the time and felt she left only because the "right" person was on the way. After a month of waiting, nothing had happened. I had given my inner guide all the help I could, but was still alone.

I was in France, camping on a small island in a most romantic setting amid fishing villages and vineyards. As I sat wondering why I was still alone, I thought, " *What a shame it is to waste this beautiful adventure.*" I wondered also why my inner guide did not get busy and send me someone to share it.

This particular evening, I was drinking a glass of wine and watching the sunset. My guide was silent. Not one word or thought came to me about my perfect mate, though I continued to ask. My thoughts were filled with my loneliness. I was bothered by some small birds that kept flying very near my face. Several times they came so close that I ducked since it appeared they would hit me. I thought, *"What are these crazy birds doing?"* My inner guide said, *"They are making love to you."* It was the first time he'd spoken that evening and the idea seemed ridiculous in the beginning. However, I was willing to consider anything.

As I thought about the idea, it began to seem possible. Despite not finding my perfect mate, I'd been having some very unusual experiences. I allowed the tiny birds' attentions to comfort me. Now, I viewed their antics in a whole new light.

As I allowed myself to feel this love and support, a very unusual thing happened. The trees and the bushes around me also began to send me love. It is very hard to describe. It was like waves or shimmers of color and light moving around me. It appeared much like the distortion you see on a very hot day as heat waves radiate on a highway blurring the landscape.

This was no vision, but an actual experience, a warm comforting feeling of love and connection with everything around me. It was quite a shock since only moments before I had felt all alone and deserted. I could clearly see everything was made of love. Love was the essence and nature of everything. It was the basic element of creation--like seeing atoms and knowing they were love. I felt connected to everything.

I remember thinking how foolish I had been in my search for love. I could not find love in a world made totally of love. I felt like a starving caveman suddenly transported to a supermarket and unable to find food since he knew nothing of packaging. I, too, was fooled by the containers of love all about me and unable to see the nourishment inside. If love did not come in the package I wanted -- a certain height, weight, and appearance -- I had rejected it.

Next I saw myself as a lonely king in a heavily guarded castle high on a mountain top. Each time I had been disappointed by a visitor who brought a gift to my castle,

I had closed the castle's huge wooden gates a little more. I had had so many visitors that now the gates were shut tight. No one could get in. I was locked up inside peering out through the cracks, wondering if I would be visited again. I knew I was starving to death in that fortress.

I resolved to throw the gates open and let everyone in. I would keep no thing out regardless of species, size, sex, age, weight, shape, or attractiveness. I realized that my castle had been locked so tightly that only a tiny bird could get in. Oh, the love I felt for those wonderful, brave birds.

I decided to accept love from everyone and everything in the world, no exceptions. The next day, I was very excited to go out and find the many forms of love. My life changed that day. Everyone seemed eager to help and know me. The world was bright and shining. No, I did not meet the "girl of my dreams" right away. That was to happen nearly seven years later. In fact, before that happened, I had to decide there might never be that special woman and that I could be content alone. I had to decide that my relationship with God was my number one relationship, but that's a story for another time.

For the next week, my life which had been quite lonely was filled with loving people. It was so full that I had to ask my inner guide for a few days alone. This loving connection was great, but just too intense for someone used to being locked up in a fortress. I had not learned yet to say "no" and to honor my own feelings and desires.

I also asked my guide for some physical contact. I wanted sex and companionship, but was willing to settle for just a hug if that could be arranged. I felt pretty sure I was not ready for a girlfriend, but I did need more than just conversation.

A few days later, I was setting up my tent in a campsite in central France along a lovely small stream. As I hammered in the tent pegs, I was aware of something running toward me. I glanced up to see a small black animal coming my way. *"What a strange looking dog,"* I thought. I glanced up again as it got closer and thought it was a long-legged, rather large cat. The next thing I knew, it was coming straight for me and, grasping my leg, it climbed up into my arms. It turned out to be a little girl monkey and her hugs were truly heaven-sent.

For the next three days whenever she saw me, she pulled up her little stake and chain and ran to hug me. Despite her owner's apologies and dismay at her actions, our love affair continued. This lonely traveler will long remember fondly those tiny hugs.

That is not the end of the story. About a week later, my daughter, Elese, joined me and we spent a month traveling together and getting reacquainted. After my first divorce, she had lived with her mother and my son had eventually come to live with me. We had not spent a long time together since she was little, due primarily to the divorce and then to the fact that she now lived in Europe. During the next month, we had many opportunities to discuss in depth all the hurts which were caused by the divorce. Since she had also recently gone through a divorce, it was a very healing experience for both of us and very timely.

I had been looking for a girlfriend when my daughter proposed coming along on my trip for a month. I knew her presence would make finding a lover impossible, but I welcomed the time we could be together. At the end of our joint travels, my daughter took a train to Paris to resume her studies. After saying goodbye, I was leaving the train station when my inner guide said loudly, *"Now which would you choose?"* I knew what that meant. I had been looking for the perfect mate to complete my life. Instead I had been given a wonderful and most important reunion with my daughter. It was a period of laughter, sharing, and understanding which I could not have planned. Had I gotten my wish for a girlfriend to accompany me, the opportunity to spend time with my daughter would not have occurred. I realized I really did not know what was best for anyone, but if I was willing to give up trying to get love **my way**, what was best would happen.

The Truth Comes Out

Another breakthrough occurred as I loosened my tight grip on the idea that I knew what I needed in terms of love. A few evenings later, I was told in guidance what I had been doing that caused me to have so many unsatisfactory relationships. The **problem** was caused by something I believed about myself; something I had kept hidden even from my consciousness. When I first saw it, it was so hateful I could only feel disgust. I now see it as a silly idea with no real consequence except to bring me pain as long as I believed it.

In every relationship, I had chosen someone I thought really needed me and the qualities I had to offer. I thought my lover's dependency would guarantee her love and loyalty. By providing what my lover needed, I reasoned she would appreciate what I had given and would give me the love and support I needed in return. What I looked for was someone who was dependent on my ability to provide stability, support, and comfort. Unfortunately, I never told her what I was doing or even admitted it to myself. I made a hidden bargain or contract. It read like this, *"I will provide you with security, support, and protection from your fears. In return, you will provide me with the love, special attention, and complete loyalty that I need"*.

Of course, I assumed she not only knew what I needed, but agreed to provide it in return for what I was doing. I never told anyone of this bargain, but I held my partner firmly bound to every clause. I kept track of each violation of the agreement and when the agreement was broken too severely in my judgment, I would leave the relationship without explanation. Seeing this, I was repulsed at how sneaky, selfish, and proud I had been. I had called this love, but it was not love -- it was a contract. I had not even told the other party such an agreement was in force, nor had they consented to abide by its terms. My contract not only violated God's Law of Love which gives without any expectation, but it violated the world's legal system which requires that a contract be open and agreed to by all parties.

Worst of all, I was always very self-righteous about my illegal contract when it was broken. I would say,

"Look at all I did for her and how she did not appreciate it." Best of all, my friends agreed too. YUCK! It was so ugly. How could I have done that and not realized what I was doing? I hated me at that moment.

Then I was told lovingly by my inner guide that I had only made a mistake. It was all right. I was trying to find love in the wrong way; it wasn't bad. What I was doing simply would not work. I was also told it was important that I attempt to get love this way for as long as I believed it would work. I needed to find out that my illegal contract was based on a false assumption. The assumption I made about myself that caused me to seek love this way was that I was not lovable as I **am**. I believed and assumed that I was not valuable as myself; only if I offered something of additional value would I be lovable. Thus I thought unless I offer my strength and protection or something the other person needs, she will not love me. I believed in conditional love. It was love based on mutual **need**, a system in which each partner provides what the other seeks. It was a mutual attempt to **earn** love. The term "co-dependency" is often used to describe this type of relationship. A better term would be "mutual neediness." This is not Love and does not work.

Unlike the birds who offer their song to all and the trees who offer shade to everything, I only offered love conditionally and only accepted love conditionally. I was told by my inner guide, *"Love does not have to be earned. Love Is."*

I had been told over and over that God loved me. Now, I knew what that meant. He loves me without conditions, as I **am**. He does not ever require me to earn

His Love. If I wanted to experience Love in its true and only nature, I also had to be willing to love others and myself without conditions, agreements, or bargains. Love as a natural state requires no other additions. Love is complete in itself. Love is perfect.

Three Steps That Uncover False Beliefs

Answers concerning our core beliefs may not come immediately since we are seldom willing to question our basic concepts. Our projections are made to protect these false core beliefs. They are simply misperceptions and false limitations which we believe about ourselves.

In the process of uncovering these false concepts, the **First Step** is to receive the **signal**. These signals usually come in the form of feelings of distress or upset and notify us that our concepts are not bringing us the desired results. We must honestly admit we are getting a message. *"Yes, I Am Upset About This."* The temptation is to ignore the signal and try again to make our false concept work with someone else. If we substitute, we simply delay the process. We cannot avoid a signal forever because each time we receive it and ignore it, the signal (often pain) gets louder.

The **Second Step** is to be open and willing to have the truth revealed to us. We do this by **not** holding someone else responsible and by **"accepting"** what is happening. Someone else is not responsible, no matter how it seems. Our distress is caused by our own false beliefs and the limitations we are putting on ourselves. We need to be willing to have them revealed even if they are ugly and scary. In time we will find that these limitations and beliefs are not true. They will become silly ideas that are no longer important. We will have our freedom. We do not have to fix ourselves up. We will find we are perfect as we are, now. It may seem impossible, but the realization of this perfection will come. **"Listening"** is the process that reveals false beliefs and concepts. Once revealed and seen clearly, the false belief will vanish. We do not remove false beliefs.

The **Third Step** is to wait for the clarity. Just keep hearing the signals and spend time **"listening"** within for clarity. It will come to us at the right time. We do not have to dig around for it. During this period gratitude for the person pushing our buttons will help to speed up the process. Each time we think of them, we try to think of something we admire or appreciate about them. This opens our minds so we can **"accept."**

We Move Straight At The Problem

It is helpful here to suspend our judgment of what is happening. We must be willing to look at something that may seem disgusting and terrifying. We have to seek the truth about ourselves, even if it seems fearful to do so. We are trying to move beyond our little mind's belief system to our perfection. We are not trying to ignore the core belief but uncover it. The direction is not away from the seeming problem, but straight at it and through it. As we move toward the seeming problem, we will begin to see things clearly. To go past the false belief, we must not react to it. We just acknowledge it and continue to be willing to **"listen"** to our inner guide who knows the way.

During this **Second Step**, the **uncovering**, it is not necessary to see the false belief clearly, but merely to be willing to have the Truth revealed. In fact, it is impossible to see the belief clearly at this stage. This is important; we often try to figure things out before we move past them or turn them over. It will not work.

Not A "Figure-it-Out" Exercise

If we stop to "figure-it-out" or fix the problem, we become lost in it. Fixing the problem at the level of the problem, at the level it seems real, will only change the problem's appearance and will not bring real freedom. We cannot change our concept of our limited nature alone, but we can become willing to release the attraction to the idea which causes the problem and move beyond it. This feels more like **letting go** of some idea or belief than changing it.

Moving Past Limitation

If we move beyond the concept of limitation, even for only a moment, we can experience our unbroken connection with the Divine. This **Third Step** in the relinquishment of perception requires little on our part. It is accomplished by following the **"listening"** process and stilling or quieting our mind. In the third step, we are willing to open to guidance. **"Listening,"** we move past our sense of limitation and see problems as concepts and beliefs that did not work. We move beyond a desire to change others, ourselves, or events. We become grateful for others as they are and for the blessings they have given us. We see that our past beliefs and actions, as well as the actions of others, were merely unsuccessful attempts which did not bring the desired results.

Seeing this clearly, what else can we do but stop doing what is not working? Seeing we do not know what to do or what will work, we are now open to following inner guidance. We quietly await its sure arrival at the right time and place.

Our Will Must Be Joined With God's Will

We cannot attain this level of "**acceptance**" by using our will alone, no matter how much we desire change. What is needed is a perception shift and to see with new eyes. This can only occur as we join our will with God's Will. Our inner guide is always leading us gently to this union. We do not give up our will in abject surrender, for that never works. We must desire to be a full partner in the awakening process. We express our willingness to join with the Divine Will by seeking this union above all else. This joining will occur naturally when we want nothing else. There is no other way.

Hanging By My Fingernails

Just before I moved to the Retreat, I traveled a great deal with a dear friend and companion. She taught me many lessons; one I will never forget involves the joining of my will with God's Will. We were driving in Basel, Switzerland, trying to find a Chinese Restaurant we knew was near the center of town. I have driven in this city on several occasions and have had no trouble finding my way. In fact, finding my way with inner guidance was something I was very proud of before this event.

On this day, no matter which direction I turned, I remained lost and confused. I wanted my friend to help me, but said nothing to her. What I really wanted was for her to **want** to help without my asking. I became more and more upset as she calmly fixed her fingernails.

I tried to let my frustration go and to forgive her, but it did not work.

Finally, being out of patience, I asked her to help me by looking at the road signs and our map. Taking little thought and not consulting the map, she pointed out a road up ahead and said, *"Go that way."* She then returned to filing her nails and enjoying herself. One of my issues with her was that she did not participate with or support me in the way I wanted. She was teaching me the lesson of honoring myself, but at this point I did not get it. I grew more and more upset as we drove along and listed silently to myself all the grievances I had against her. The road seemed to go further and further into the country, away from downtown. I thought, *"I'll show her the consequences of not helping me; I'll keep driving on this road even if we end up in Zurich."*

She continued to fix her nails, undisturbed. I alone was getting more and more upset. The anger grew way out of proportion to the small event that was happening. Finally, I realized, *"She's fine; she's doing what she wants and enjoying this ride. I'm the only one who is upset. I'm just hurting myself. How silly! What am I trying to prove?"* I saw the utter stupidity of what I was doing.

I had many other options besides getting mad at her. I could ask her for more help, I could stop and ask directions, or I could simply look at the map myself. I was just being miserable to prove a point and then holding her responsible for my pain. It was not working because I was the only one in pain. Right then and there I gave it up. *"I am willing to follow your guidance,*

God. Take me where You will; I do not care." I thought to myself.

As if by magic, a sign popped up out of nowhere pointing to the right and clearly marked Centrum (meaning center). I turned, left the country road and drove onto a freeway which put us downtown in a few minutes. As I pulled into the central area, I found a free parking space. I felt we might be near the restaurant and, since parking spaces were impossible to find at any time and especially during the lunch hour, I grabbed it willing to walk the rest of the way. As I got out of the car, I looked across the street and there was the restaurant. My friend smiled knowingly as if she had planned the whole thing. Maybe she did! *"When will I ever learn?"*, I thought to myself.

Letting Go Of Our Blankees

When we learn that what we want does not bring us our heart's desire, we are no longer controlled by it. When you were young, you may have had a blanket you loved. In time, it became dirty and ragged, but you would not give it up. If it was taken away you probably replaced it with something else. A teddy bear or a doll. That too you may now have outgrown. (Don't worry if you have not, we all keep teddy bears in some form or other.) As long as you needed your teddy bear to be happy, it had power over you. The object may be removed, but while the need remains, it will create desires for other things.

I would guess you have grown to a point where you do not want your blanket back. You do not see it as necessary to your happiness. Therefore it has no power over you. In fact, if you had to carry a blanket around all day, you would find it embarrassing. You do not desire it because you do not see it as useful in your daily life. At this point, your happiness is not controlled by your blanket. This **outgrowing** is the only way to move past or heal false concepts.

We Do Not Change, We Outgrow

This is how we move past all of our limitations. A **blankee** is a limitation or something we need to be happy. In time we see that the thing no longer makes us happy. Then we gladly put the **blankee** down with no thought of sacrifice; it is no longer useful. We can do this with any belief that is limiting. You might say we are healed of the dependency. If we replace our need for a **blankee** with the need for a lover, we are still controlled. We still find our happiness controlled by something outside ourselves. Only the form has changed. We usually substitute one dependency with another rather than release the need. The chosen substitution may be more acceptable to us, at the time, but it does nothing to eliminate the limitation.

Giving Up Our Blankees Doesn't Work

Whenever we sacrifice something we think we need, give up something we want but see as harmful, or desire something harmful but force ourselves to avoid it, we remain controlled by it. It may be helpful on a temporary basis to avoid things that do great damage to us, but the real healing occurs only when we no longer desire them. We cannot willfully give up the **blankees** we want and not be affected by it. We can grow to a point in our awareness where we no longer see their usefulness and eagerly discard them. This is the only real freedom from the limitation.

Using Our Will To Shorten Time

We are not asked to give up what we want. That is not the message from our unlimited Divine Source. Desires for what is limited will never satisfy us and will only control and thereby limit us for a while. We will always outgrow limitations, since we are in Reality unlimited. Desire for what is unlimited can never be given up. The good news is that any limited concept will eventually self-destruct. That is, it will have no power over us when we outgrow it.

What Is Real Is Eternal And Never Changes. What Is Not, Vanishes When We Withdraw Our Belief In It's Reality and Usefullness.

This is the process of God's Will. Nothing else happens. In time this process may seem very long and extremely painful. It seems long because of the intensity of our desires and painful because of our perceived needs and cherished fantasies. We can shorten this process. We can always choose again.

This is the purpose of time as our inner guide uses it. We are not forced to give up our **blankees**. We are lovingly given all the time we want to outgrow them. *Isn't That Wonderful!* Can we do less than extend this loving concept to everyone else, since we are all struggling with our current favorite **blankees**? In this cycle of seeking and never finding, we will never discover a **blankee** (limitation) that will satisfy us. The outcome is always certain . . . we are unlimited.

Moving Beyond The Comfort Level

In the beginning, it may feel like a loss as we outgrow our addictions or needs. That is because part of us clings to the familiar and feels concern regarding the new. The new is often uncomfortable. It is like coming into the sunlight from a dark cave; our human minds and senses need time to adjust. However, as we more fully realize that the old needs were not helpful, we will begin to feel a lightness.

Even in the beginning, as we start to release these limitations, we have a deep inner feeling of following the right path despite missing what is comfortable. We know a burden has been lifted from us as we move along. Remembering honestly the pain that our old needs and limitations created will help us during this adjustment period. The longing for the old will only continue until we see we have given up nothing.

Recognizing Our Will

The belief that we have to give up our heart's desires to follow guidance is false. In fact, we must use our will (heart's desire) to follow inner guidance. We are always using our will. We should never try to, and cannot really, ever give it up. We can try to suspend it, but it will surface in time. The Divine part of us will not let us be imprisoned. We are always free to seek what we desire. That is our will.

To see what is your will, just look around you. What is happening to you is **your will**. Your will is bringing your experiences to you and determining how you perceive them. If you are affirming abundance and wishing for it, but you are experiencing deprivation, **your will** is to experience poverty.

Seeing this, we can choose to dedicate ourselves to following inner guidance and, by using our will, make this dedication a reality. Why would we wish to have poverty if we knew we had the choice to have abundance? Let's answer that question next and see how we create our concept of reality, which is really a duality.

Chapter 6

REALITY AND DUALITY

WHY DO WE EXPERIENCE LIMITATION?

We have chosen a limited existence because poverty, distrust, powerlessness, and hatred match the picture we have deep inside of who we are and who we want to be. To feel separate, we have to choose to feel other than abundance, connection, oneness, and love. Why do we choose to be limited beings? Because we desire to separate ourselves from our Divine Source which is unlimited. To have an individual experience, we must desire to feel unconnected or to experience Reality other than it is. We have literally sought to create our own little being separate from the Creator and the rest of creation. We have convinced ourselves that this existence is Reality. It is not.

By making this choice, we seemed to separate ourselves from abundance, love, and limitlessness. We cannot experience being both separate and unlimited. By separating and individualizing, we chose to experience limitedness. We may experience both love and hate, or poverty and abundance at times in this duality, but we will not experience only love, abundance, and limitlessness. Unless we experience **only** this, we are experiencing the illusion of love, abundance, and limitlessness and not their Reality.

I asked my inner guide to explain how this illusion can have such a hold on our minds, since it is unreal. This is the illustration he gave me.

The Monkey Story

He said, *"They catch monkeys in the Orient with a simple device. They use a basket with a small opening and place a piece of fruit inside the basket. They then tie the basket to a stake. The monkey comes along and reaches into the basket to get the fruit. As he makes a fist and holds onto his prize, his paw becomes too large to get out of the basket. The men then come along and pick up the monkey. He is trapped by his beliefs. There is nothing else holding him. He can easily get away if he lets go of the fruit. But, he will not let go. What traps him is the concept, If I let go, I will lose something.*

I was told that this same concept traps us. **We feel if we let go of what we have -- our limited self -- we will lose something.** So we hold on tight to our identity or ego, and we are trapped. If we let go, which is scary because we are not sure what will happen, we are free. We find we have lost nothing but gained our true identity, unlimitedness. My guide then quipped, *"Don't let your ego make a monkey out of you. Be willing to let go of your identity!"*

The Fear Of Reality

Do you find it hard to believe that you fear Reality and are afraid to let go of all your concepts? Are you willing to let go of your identity, especially the parts you think of as **good**? Think of your fear of meeting God face-to-face. Can you feel your fear of losing your little self to something bigger? I got in touch with this basic fear while traveling in Europe in 1983.

I was in England near Falmouth, staying in a small inn. I had been thinking a great deal about meeting and seeing the Christ face-to-face. I had been reading "A Course In Miracles," which seemed to be stating that this was possible. That night I was awakened suddenly at about 2 a.m. by my inner guide and was told to go down the hall to the bathroom. There he said I would meet the Christ. Despite the fact that I had been asking and hoping for just such an event, I was too terrified to leave the safety of my bed.

It took me nearly ten minutes to get up the courage to go down the hall. I realized for the first time my fear of facing the Truth. The thought that most terrified me was that I would have no secrets; that I could hide nothing and Jesus Christ would see all my mistakes and judge me as very unworthy. With great trembling, I finally opened the bathroom door and turned on the light. The room was empty. My first reaction was relief. My second reaction was great disappointment at being so afraid and missing a wonderful opportunity. I returned to bed but slept little.

I felt humble and sad for the next two days and vowed that, if given a second chance, I would not fail. On the third day, it came to me.... the bathroom was the only place in the house that had a **mirror**! I remembered looking at myself in the bathroom mirror the evening of my **missed** encounter, and hating myself. At that time I could only see a failure in that mirror, **an ugly, scared failure.**

Seeing The Christ

That night I spent some time in front of another mirror trying to see the Christ in me. Over the next seven months, my lessons were all involved with seeing the Christ everywhere and in everyone, especially myself.

It was most helpful to touch the stark terror we all have at really seeing the Truth. Christ means my real being. Christ is the name of my true self. Only a few people have glimpsed the magnitude of this concept and been willing to embrace and experience it.

Jesus was one who fully embodied the concept of Christ and demonstrated that we are Divine, here and now. Many false ideas have been expounded about who he was and what he did. Do not let another's prejudice keep you from finding the great Truth contained in his life and his message. Many others have embodied the Christ ideal, some to a great extent and some partially. They have various names and different ways of expressing the message. Some may appeal to you more than others and that is fine. The names and descriptive phrases do not really matter. Only the concept of our union with the Divine is important.

What matters is that each one of us realizes he and she are God's offspring. We can fully demonstrate we are created by a Divine Power and we can express that Divinity here and now. That is Reality. The power of expressing that Divinity here and now is available to all who use their will and want nothing else. In fact, when we stop trying to be something else, we naturally express our Divinity. It is not something to do, but something that is, when we stop doing.

What's Love Got To Do With It?

Most of us want to love others and all of us want to be loved. Why then do we experience a life of feeling so alone? It is because our powerful will and our desire to be separate overrides what would be our natural state of joining with everyone and everything. Instead of the experience of Love, which is natural Oneness, our will brings us what we expect -- loneliness and separation. Separation is what we really ask for when we do not trust others and do not extend love to everything.

We only have to look at our experience to see what we truly **will**. This is the good news; Our life is a wonderful gauge telling us what we truly desire, despite our efforts to fool ourselves. When you are experiencing something you do not like, it is because you have willed to have it and believe it is what you deserve.

For example, say you experience being lonely or not finding someone you truly love. How do you change that? Do you search for someone you can love? No. Why? Because to find one person to love goes against the very essence of what Love is. Love is not Love if it is directed at only one person. It may be passion, possession, or a special relationship, but it's not God's Love which is the only real Love.

Finding Love Through Use Of Our Will

How then do we find love? We remember one of God's Laws. What you give, you receive. If we want to receive love, we first need to give it. Since Love is not special, if it is real, we seek to give love to everyone. Does that mean we are intimate with everyone? No, closeness, intimacy, and sex are not love. The illusions of love called sex, companionship, intimacy, and closeness are often selfishness, neediness, possession and control. Love means we see everyone as deserving of our respect and we honor them. We treat them as we wish to be treated. That is Love. From this place

81

of expressing real Love, we are open to receiving it and it will come of its own Grace.

Our inner guide will send us the people we need, at the times we need them. Our job, using our will properly, is to not reject people because they do not match our pictures of love. Does that mean we have to make everyone a dear friend? No. It means we are open to receiving from everyone the gifts they bring. Then we return these gifts by honoring and loving them. That is the purpose of gratitude. That is learning that giving and receiving are one. **"Accepting"** each person is the way we express Love as it truly is. **"Accepting"** is Love demonstrated.

What if someone tells us they are guided to be our partner, mate, or lover? If we hear the same guidance, fine. Let's assume, however, that we do not share their desires in this regard. We can still love and respect them, even if we do not feel guided to join in a special relationship with them. Why? Because we must love and honor ourselves as well as others. Being where we do not want to be or sacrificing our needs and desires is not loving ourselves.

If we are not inner-guided to be in a certain intimate relationship, we can still share a loving relationship with that person and everyone else. This relationship may be to honor and respect them. It may even involve telling them no, but not withdrawing from them. We approach sex and intimacy the same way. When sex is an expression of love shared between two people and it honors both partners, it expresses Divine Love and will bring joy and satisfaction. When sex is used not to love and honor, but to control, possess, or get, it is not Love and will not satisfy. It is simply pleasure but it is not Love. All material pleasures are temporary, eventually disappointing and failing us.

Don't Assume You Know Love

For specific answers regarding Love, only your inner guide can instruct you on what is the most loving action. You can be guided to say and do the best thing in every circumstance. Your only desire needs to be; to be an expression of Divine Love. Ask by going within concerning what to do and say. You need only desire to love everyone, including yourself, and to follow guidance even if it does not match your human pictures of Love. If this is your true desire, you will be led to the right action. Often the problem will simply dissolve or solve itself in a wonderful way. When you are **"accepting"** everyone involved, that is usually all you need to do.

Changing Our Will Changes Our Experiences

Since our will brings our experiences, as we change our will our experiences change. This also happens when we use affirmations or visualization. They work because our will is very powerful. However, mind control methods bring incomplete results because they are being directed by a limited mind, as we have discussed. They have no other power or magic potion except that given by your belief. I caution you about their use, since their results can be disappointing.

You can choose (will) something you think might make you happy, but do you know what truly makes you happy? In our present state, we are like very powerful children. Like young, uneducated children, we think we know but we do not understand what is really going on. If we join our limited mind which has a long list of things it thinks will make us happy, with our powerful will, we will often get these things. But we still will not be happy. That is because we do not know what makes us truly happy.

I know many people who have visualized their perfect mate or perfect job or perfect something and gotten it, only to find they left out some very important requirements. That is why we must join our will or desires with God's Will and Direction. We do this by following inner guidance. Without this joining, we can only experience limited results. This is why what we desire and then get never satisfies us except in one instance. If we desire union with our Divine Source, above all else, then we will get it. From this union all else we need is provided naturally.

How To Set Goals

How does it work to join our will through inner guidance with God's Will? Let us say we have a specific goal in mind, something we desire which we think would make us happy. Is that wrong? No. It is almost impossible not to have preferences in every situation. In fact, setting a goal is often helpful because it gives us a stated direction and clearly identifies what we think we need. In effect, it shows us what we really want. The important thing is not to make this goal a god. It is merely a starting place. We should remain open and willing to change direction or goals at any time when so led by inner guidance. This is why an attitude of "**accepting**" is vital to following inner guidance and setting goals.

As we proceed toward our goal, we check our thoughts and our experience. Is this going smoothly? Are we enjoying it? Are we getting crazy over some timetable or a particular item? Are doors closing and other doors opening? Do I need to continue ahead or change direction? Am I in an open and "**accepting**" frame of mind or am I struggling to bring something about? If you are open to guidance, you will know when it is time to change direction or goals.

Are We Guided Or Forcing Things?

The most important question, one that cannot be asked too often is, "Am I being guided to do this?" Stated another way, "Is this my plan or God's plan?"

We are powerful beings, even in our present illusionary state. Giving up our willpower is not asked, required, or helpful. Our will can be misused and bring us pain. Pain will eventually bring the realization that we need to change what we are doing. The answer is to **never** give up our power. Our will is a gift from God. He is sharing His creativeness with us by giving us free will. However, without inner guidance, we separate this creative power from Love, Wisdom, Truth, and Joy. Is it any wonder our will can bring us painful experiences?

Asking About Everything

Early on, I asked my inner guide why I needed to follow his guidance, exclusively as he had requested. I had been successful making decisions and felt it was rather a put-down to be told to always ask about everything. Had my past decisions been so terrible that they could not be trusted? Was I really that incompetent? I was told, "*You have made many good decisions and I know you try to do the best for yourself and others most of the time. However, you need my guidance in everything because you do not value yourself as highly as I do.*" That shocked me, I have never thought of myself as overly modest.

My guide continued, "*You are like a starving man who sneaks into a large banquet. You steal a small finger sandwich and rearrange the tray so that no one will know. Then you sneak away before anyone sees, you hide in the alley, and eat your meager meal. Little do you know it was a banquet in your honor. Everyone was waiting for you to arrive.*"

That example changed my view of inner guidance. I no longer saw it as an intrusion on what I wanted. I saw it was a way to get what I truly deserved. I knew what I had been told was true, though it was hard to believe. My experiences since then are that I am **always** better cared for by inner guidance than by my own efforts. My life has indeed become a banquet and I no longer settle for finger sandwiches as I have done in the past.

How To Make The Right Decision

My guide then added, "*There is another advantage in always following inner guidance in everything. It blesses everyone involved. You may not always see it, but if you have tried to '**listen**' as best you can, your decisions will be blessed.*"

He asked, "*Have you not struggled over your decisions trying to please everyone? Have you ever been successful?*" I had to admit I had often struggled to please everyone and also that I had never been completely successful. Someone always seemed to have been left out. Often it was me.

He said, *"Following my guidance, you will never have to worry. I know everyone's needs that will be touched by your decision. All will be given what they need if you will only do as I guide you. You may not see it right away or ever, but you can trust that this is always happening."* To the best of my knowledge, that has been true. I have seen many instances of how this works. The Retreat is certainly one. I am very glad to give up the burden of doing the **right thing** and making the **right decision**. All I have to do is follow what I am inner-directed to do; not perfectly, just to the best of my ability.

The Apartment

That sounds easy, doesn't it? Simply follow inner guidance and you will make the right decision. But it's not always evident that you have made the right decision. When guidance goes against our core beliefs, it is not easy to recognize it. Several years ago, I had a chance to really see this principle in operation.

I was renting a small apartment in front of my house to my son and his girlfriend. I was in the process of remodelling it and so I rented it to him for very little money. I planned to get more rent in the future, since my first trip to Europe was dependent on having my property self-sufficient. I did not have the time or money then to fix the place up, so my son, Brian, continued to rent the apartment at a low rate.

My other apartment was suddenly vacant and so I advertised for a new renter. A nice young couple came who loved the location, but said the available apartment was too small. They asked if I had something else. I said, *"I do have one I'm working on and which my son rents, but it will not be available for some time."* They wanted to see it and, on seeing it, fell in love with it. I was reticent to make any commitment. I was torn between my need to make full rent and my desire to help Brian.

I was following inner guidance at this time and felt they were sent to me. However, I could not get clarity on what to do. I sent them away saying, *"If you can't find anything else in a couple of weeks, call me."* I had learned, when in doubt about guidance, I should wait, ask within, and look for more signs.

One of the signs I used then to determine if I was getting inner guidance was the recurrence of something three times within a short period. When something repeated three times, I then knew I was hearing correctly. I was sure the couple would not call unless they were meant to come to the apartment. Meanwhile, my other place was still vacant and I was running short of money. I could not figure out why my guide did not get busy and rent the vacant apartment thereby solving my problems simply.

Two weeks later, the couple called and still wanted the apartment. They even offered more rent than what I was asking. I stalled again. Despite problems with Brian and his girlfriend, I could not bring myself, as a good father, to tell them they had to leave. Every time I went inside to ask, I thought I heard my inner guide tell me that my son was to leave. I doubted that such a message would be guidance, however, since it did not appear loving.

The couple called again. This was number three and my last excuse faded. I had told them I had no time or money to fix up the apartment. They said their father would do all the work and they would pay for it. I knew something was happening. I asked Brian to move out and explained I needed to get full rent so I could go to Europe. I offered him the vacant apartment, but this time for nearly the full rental price as directed by guidance.

During the many years we had been living together, Brian and I had been very close. He had never been the problem most teenage sons are. However, both he and his girlfriend became very hostile about the move and would hardly talk to me. They rented the other apartment for several months and then broke up. Brian blamed me for all his problems and especially the trouble he was having with his girlfriend. Our relationship was shattered and I was deeply hurt by the loss of our closeness.

I left for Europe several months later, feeling I had followed inner guidance but it had caused me to lose my great relationship with my son. I was feeling very confused about the situation. I did not like the results of following this particular guidance. All the other guidance had produced positive effects in my life. This was not positive in my view. I hoped time would heal this problem and I doubted that I had heard to do the right thing.

On my return, Brian called and suggested we have lunch. During our meeting, he said, *"You know Dad about the apartment..."* I cut him off and stated I did not want to talk about that problem anymore. He said.

"No Dad, it's not a problem. It was the best thing you ever did for me." As the story unfolded, he reported that he and his girlfriend had been using drugs and that the money they saved on rent let them buy what they needed. When they had to pay full rent, there was no money for such activity and his girlfriend had left. As a result, he stopped using any type of stimulants and became very active in the Christian Youth Revival. Now he devotes a great deal of time to his church, has matured into a fine young man, and married a lovely girl who shares his deep faith in God.

Since the **Apartment** episode, I have seen a dramatic change in Brian's attitude toward life and his determination to learn and grow. He was always a most loving and spiritual person, but now his willingness to put all his efforts into a new life are outstanding.

Knowing You Don't Know

My inner guide knew what I could not know. It was important that my concept of a "loving father" did not interfere with the direction I was getting from inner guidance. I have come to realize that I do not know what "truly loving" looks like. I must be willing to give up all my concepts even of love and rely solely on inner guidance for my direction. I cannot look to the world, other persons, or my past experiences for agreement with what I hear to do. The outside world will never agree with inner guidance. If it did we would not need guidance.

We have discussed the use of problems as **signals** that we have limited beliefs. We realize our will is holy and brings us all we need. Now, let's examine how all things can be perceived as **blessings**.

Chapter 7

"ACCEPTING" PUTS GUIDANCE INTO PRACTICE

"Accepting" Reveals The Power Of "Listening"

The full use of the process of **"listening"** is not merely the development of techniques for receiving information from a higher source. Nor is it merely using this information to correct various aspects of one's life or to understand what is happening. These are merely first steps which make us aware of the potential of **"listening."** They are, however, steps that must be experienced until we are confident that we can ask about anything and get an immediate response.

In the process of **"listening,"** we learn to go past the information we receive from our worldly mind and to become still. It becomes natural to spend time during the day receiving information from our higher source. We develop a natural reaction of being still and **"listening"** whenever we become upset or angry. Great benefits occur as we extend this process to every facet of our daily lives and to all aspects of our thinking. We find **"listening"** is opening doors for us and guiding us easily to what makes us truly happy.

As we begin to **"accept"**, we see that all things are guidance, regardless of their form. For example, if we wish to do something and do not have the money to do it, we see this as guidance. We realize it must not be time for this activity and we wait for clarity to come. When it comes, we know we are to proceed. If the money or whatever does not come, we discover a different path opening before us.

"Accepting" Changes Conflict To Perfection

"Accepting" changes our perspective of ourselves and the world. No longer is the world a place of conflict and danger. No longer are we potential victims of circumstances. All things become part of the plan for our happiness, regardless of the form they take. Sickness, stress, and accidents become **signals** that we need to turn within and **"listen."**

We do not seek to cure or change anything; we see everything coming to help and bless us. We start from the standpoint that all is perfect, including ourselves. Perfect just as it is appearing. Our only job is to **"accept"** what is and seek clarity as needed. Things or events are not lessons or trials, they are simply part of the guidance we are receiving and we can welcome not resist them.

From this standpoint of **"accepting"** and **"listening,"** we begin to look out from our perfect being on perfect events and perfect brothers and sisters. It is not necessary that they realize their perfection, but only that **we** do. As we see this, we will find the world transformed into a loving and beautiful place created for our joy and happiness. From this place we begin to perceive that we are not human beings but spiritual beings. We see that we are unlimited, eternal, and invulnerable. The old concepts begin to fall away and we see, not duality or separation, but Oneness and connectedness.

"Accepting" Lets Us "Listen" Properly

"Accepting" is the only way to move beyond a world of conflict and pain to a world of love and joy. If we use **"listening"** to get information on how to fix the world or others, including ourselves, we will remain trapped in a dualistic concept of pain and joy, light and darkness, and love and hate. We will think that our job here is to fix the one and support the other. We will run around trying to heal and help and, in the end, find our efforts not appreciated and not effective.

When we move to the attitude of "**accepting**," we know all is perfect and part of God's plan. We do not see two possibilities, but only one. That one is always God's perfect plan unfolding perfectly. Now we "**listen**," not to change the world or ourselves, **but to experience the world and ourselves as perfect.**

Starting from a standpoint of perfection, which we reach by "**accepting**," we can now "**listen**" totally since our mind is at the same level as the message we are receiving. We find not only that all is perfect, but that we are perfect within this world. This requires little change and little doing. We see everyone giving us gifts and the world as perfectly constructed to provide what is truly needed. We change from being angry to being grateful.

Using "Listening" In All Facets Of Our Lives

Over the past 15 years since I consciously started this process, I have always felt that I was using guidance totally. Later, to my surprise, I would discover a whole aspect of my life where I was not "**listening**" at all. Usually it was an area where I thought I knew what needed to be done. This particularly happened in my battle to find a relationship. I gave up wanting a relationship hundreds of times and then waited to see when I would get my ideal relationship. Someone would come into my life to help me see a truth and I would try to make it a permanent relationship. Then I would grieve over my supposed loss when she accomplished her part and left.

The Proper Use Of Action

Doing It seems quite simple and yet it can be the most difficult part of the process. There is a part of us that believes that if we know how something works, that is enough. That's not true! Doing something well takes a great deal of dedication, commitment, and practice. Understanding something is the easy part; doing it well, however, is the only proof of mastery.

What Mastery Is

About two years ago, my inner guide suggested that I start playing golf again. I had abandoned it for 15 years because I had become too competitive about my performance to enjoy playing. My major lesson from resuming this activity, in addition to learning to just **play** golf, has been to learn the dedication that mastery requires. For example, I can read a great number of books about playing golf. I can watch video tapes and study the techniques of others. I understand the importance of keeping my eye on the ball and swinging smoothly. I know this and many other techniques. I am aware of the consequences of not following these simple rules. Yet the only way I can demonstrate what I have learned is to play golf on a golf course.

As much as I know about keeping my head still, and swinging slowly, and hitting the ball squarely, there is a part of me that can take over and does the opposite in a pressure situation. I can say to myself, *"Slow down, keep your eye on the ball and you will play well."* Then

I come to a long par four with a water hazard along one side. The wind begins to blow hard in my face and I worry about my second shot to the green. Anxiety takes over despite my best intentions. I swing extra hard and too fast. The result is a missed shot. Only my consistent demonstration of the principles proves I have mastered golf; there is no other measurement. (Just for the record I'm still trying to master golf.)

Spiritual Mastery Takes Practice

Living the principles we espouse is all-important. Understanding these principles is just the first step in the process. Too much emphasis placed on understanding instead of practicing can lead to frustration and denial because understanding is not accomplishment.

If you cannot do it well consistently, you have not attained mastery.

It is important to be aware of how we are using understanding. Are we trying to understand so we can pretend we are in control? Are we trying to understand so we will feel we can do something we cannot really do? Knowing how something works may give us a false sense of security and safety. If that knowledge is not coupled with the capacity to accomplish the task, it will not manifest consistent results and will fail when most needed.

Eliminating The Dependence On Understanding

I don't think I fully realized the impact of this concept until I began to live full-time at the Retreat in 1988. Until then, I often tried to understand why a person was doing something so that I could forgive them. This made it very hard to forgive, since it seemed impossible much of the time to understand why someone was doing what they were doing.

A good example of this was a situation my wife, Vikki, and I had in early 1990. She had until then enjoyed working with me at the Retreat and was instrumental in getting the books and records in perfect shape. She also enjoyed working with our employees, handling the promotion, and doing the public relations.

During a lecture trip, she confessed to me her growing feeling of unhappiness with her job at the Retreat. She did not know why nor did I. Frankly without her help, I saw no way for us to continue to run the Retreat Center. I tried to understand what she was telling me, but it did not make sense. All she knew was that she wanted to go to our staff meeting, put all the things to be done down in a pile and say, "*I quit.*"

Neither of us knew how we could solve this problem since there was no one else to do her job. I encouraged her to do what she felt she had to do, despite the fact that it brought up a lot of concern on my part. Shortly thereafter, she quit during a staff meeting saying, "*I'm not doing this any longer. If it is to be done, someone else will have to do it.*"

What happened next neither of us suspected. Two of our three staff members quit. At first I panicked and tried to organize the departures to give us time to replace our staff. But I heard inside, "*All is well. Do not try to hold on to anyone who needs to leave. All you need will be sent to you.*" So two people left and we all pitched in. Vikki got her job back to some extent, but said she did not mind now. What she had disliked most, though she could not put her finger on it at the time she was feeling to quit, was the mood of unhappiness which had been caused by two workers who felt guilty about leaving, but wanted to leave.

Because of Vikki's willingness to acknowledge her feelings, they got in touch with theirs. I, too, started to get in touch with the fact that I did not want to run the Retreat any more. And so from this incident came our willingness to let go of the management and turn the Retreat over to others.

In a short time, a couple whose dream it was to run a Retreat came to carry on the responsibility and we left for a trip around the world. On our return, it was evident Vikki and I were to concentrate on writing and lecturing and leave the Retreat to others. Now one year later, that couple is ready to change their relationship with the Retreat.

At present, no one knows what will happen. We do know that we have to release each other from expectations. We have to be willing to keep asking, *"What am I to do now?"* of our inner guide. We cannot get stuck in a routine simply because of a sense of obligation. Our first and **only** obligation is to God. That means we are to follow His plan for our happiness, not our own plan or someone else's plan.

I never do understand what is going on any more. All I know to do is to support each person in doing what they need and want to do and ask inside what I should do. My trying to understand will only get in the way of the beautiful unfoldment. As I am able to stay supportive and fairly peaceful through these changes, I begin to see the perfect activity for all involved, including me. This current major shift in our lives is the easiest one since I started **"listening,"** even though it involves a more total commitment which on occasions can bring up my fears. We are always asked to stretch a little more each time.

Understanding Is Not Forgiveness

When we understand a situation, we may feel love and compassion rather than anger. We may even believe, since we understand the situation, we have "forgiven" the other person. We may think understanding and forgiveness are the same. Yet all we demonstrate is that we will not be annoyed with another if we can find justification for their behavior. Understanding may even make us feel guilty about reacting to another doing something we do not like. We may vow not to get angry again. Yet the principle of forgiveness was never put into practice. Why? Because forgiveness does not require understanding of the situation. **"Accepting"** is forgiveness without understanding or justification.

If we require understanding to forgive, the next person who annoys us will again bring up our anger. If we don't get information that justifies their action, we may continue to be angry. We certainly won't **"accept"** what is happening and love them. Until we **"accept,"** we have not put the principle of forgiveness into action. We have only tried to understand. The only forgiveness that really works has nothing to do with understanding.

The "Accepting" Viewpoint

Forgiveness does not require us to justify what happens so we can **"accept"** it. Forgiveness that works and gives us peace recognizes that the other person is perfect. It "**accepts**" what is happening as a perfect part of the unfoldment of God's plan. It rejects all other views or opinions. It doesn't make any difference whether the situation agrees or disagrees with our plans, judgments, or concepts of how things should be. By "**accepting**", we give up the need to understand. We simply "**accept**" and love. We "**listen**" and wait for clarity to come. From an "**accepting**" viewpoint, we see all people and all activity as needing no change, correction, or even understanding on our part. All that is needed is Love.

One of the most important people we need to forgive and "**accept**" in this manner is ourselves. We do not need to understand ourselves, fix ourselves, or justify ourselves. We do need to "**accept**" ourselves as we are and then "**listen**." We should even "**accept**" the fact that it may be difficult to accept ourselves at times. Just "**accept**" that and then "**listen**."

Releasing The Need To Know

As we let go of and release the need to know and understand, we move past the idea that we can be hurt or blocked. We open to guidance which assures us we are in the right place and all is well. As we release our expectations, the **Truth that is** begins to dawn upon us. We are given Vision and Wisdom in the form of clarity and a new perspective. This is very different from **understanding**. We connect with a deep knowing which does not require information concerning the details, motives, and actions of any other person. Releasing the need to understand another, we remove the block to seeing what is at the basis of our upset about the situation. As we have stated before:

The basis of our anger or disappointment with others is always some false belief we hold concerning ourselves. This false belief sees us as limited and unlovable and is never true.

The Bleecker Story

After the founders had made the down payment and bought the Retreat Center, numerous meetings took place for the next six months. The outcome of these meetings was that we all wanted to build a Center, but we were not in agreement on the other details. I became discouraged with the lack of progress and decided to move to the Retreat site and start whatever construction was possible. There was plenty to do and little money with which to do it. I had been told by inner guidance that all we would need would be provided. There was great concern about where the walls would be, the room sizes, method of construction, financing, and so on.

One person in the group particularly bothered me --Gene Bleecker. I found out later that he was having the same experience regarding my viewpoints. We seemed to be at odds about everything, particularly the construction and design of the Retreat. It was strange because in all other ways we had the highest regard for each other and tried hard to be good friends.

The strained situation grew so bad on my part that when I knew Gene was coming to the Retreat to check on progress, I would get almost physically ill. It seemed Gene criticized everything, always suggested other ways to do things, and worst of all did not appreciate what

I was doing. I prayed for help in this matter, but could not get past my upset and my perception of how critical Gene was. If only he would change I could be happy.

Finally, in despair, I begged for help and said to my inner guide that I was willing to give up all my ideas about Gene. I just wanted my peace. To get to this state took me several months. I heard, *"Be grateful for Gene and when you think of him; think of all his good qualities."* I could try to do that.

At first, it was hard. All I could think of was how upset I felt. The first thing I thought of was that when Gene and I met for lunch we always went to nice restaurants. I could be grateful for that. I could also be grateful that he dressed nicely and acted professional. Then I remembered how kind and helpful Gene was to others. I remembered how much he loved and honored his wife. I literally clung to each **good** thing I could see about Gene as my lifeline.

As I did this I became aware that, at the Foundation meetings, it was always Gene who in the end would say something like, *"I don't agree with what Lee wants to do, but he is up there working on the building, so I think we should support him."*

I remember my surprise as I began to see this; the truth was contrary to all my complaints about Gene. It was as if I had missed what was really happening. Gene had been doing these helpful things all along, yet I had blocked them out of my awareness.

What bothered me was that he was not doing it the way I fantasized he should. Yet in the end, it was usually Gene who kept the project moving when we were stuck on opposing opinions. I became more and more grateful for his help and support. I could begin to see past the form of what I wanted to what was really happening.   I began to really appreciate Gene.

Gene has reported to me that he went through nearly the same process. I drove him crazy, too. Now we have only respect for each other. It is Gene who helped edit this book. Now I value his viewpoint greatly. I don't expect him to agree with all of my ideas, but I know without asking that I have his loyal support and unconditional love. I now recognize him as my trusted brother. Of course he always was.

I Find My Teacher At Last

During my prayers over this conflict, I read, in "A Course In Miracles",--"When the student is ready, the teacher will come." I was most anxious to know who my teacher would be. I asked my inner guide who it was and many famous names flashed in my mind as I awaited the answer. The answer was *"Gene." "You've got to be kidding,"* I thought, *"Not Gene." "Yes,"* came the reply. It was true.

Gene gave me a deep insight into one of my most cherished false beliefs. That belief is that I was lovable only if I was competent. I believed that the better I was at doing things, the more valuable I was. If I was helpful and therefore valuable, people would like and appreciate me. This was just another version of what I had learned about "identity" in my female relationships.

Like most of us, I have an enormous need for **approval**. Competency was the identity I used to get this love and approval. What I learned was that my competency had nothing to do with my value. Just as I had learned that an identity of strength and protectiveness did not make me more lovable to women. Now I saw that having to be competent and capable was not valuable but was really a prison which kept me trapped in a limited concept. I remembered God valued and loved me as perfect right now. My efforts to be competent and talented were useless attempts to get love. I do not have to prove anything or do anything to be loved. I have only to let who I am Be. What I love to do is all I need to do. When I express love and joy, I receive it.

Finding Your Teacher

What a relief! Gene helped me learn this lesson without realizing what he was doing. He did his job, as all great teachers do, by just being himself. If you want to know who your current teacher is, just look for the person right now who is rubbing you the wrong way. That's your teacher. Now be grateful and allow them to show you the truth.

Spiritual Understanding Is Not Needed

We may be willing to give up a need to understand how the world works, but can we do this with our need for spiritual understanding? Yes, it still applies. We do not have to understand how God or the Divine works. In fact, I don't believe we can know this in our present illusionary state. The Divine acts through Grace. Our understanding neither assists nor blocks the presence and activity of Grace.

Attack Disguised As Help

What we should not do is use spiritual understanding to justify our actions or to manipulate others. We should not use it to avoid taking responsibility for how we treat others. As is often wrongly said, "*I am only doing or telling you this for your own good.*"

To be specific, when we apply spiritual insights to **our own** thinking, it is very helpful. When we use spiritual insights to justify our actions or instruct others who have not requested our help, it is really an attack, no matter how loving we pretend to be. When we do this, we are saying, "*Through my superior insight, I see you as needing help and therefore less than me. I am your spiritual teacher and your anger with me is a result of YOU not being willing to accept my role. You should appreciate my suggestions and assistance in your spiritual growth.*"

That's an attack and not love. It will not make you happy except in fantasy. Each person has their own inner guide and it is not you or me. If we are to be someone's teacher without their permission, we will never be aware of it at the time.

Unrequested Advice

It is quite common for those beginning their spiritual journey to be consumed with their new **awareness**. What they are learning, they recognize as true on some level, and they assume their job is to tell everyone about it. I look back on this period in my life with some embarrassment.

The search for mistakes is easy in another person, but becomes less pleasant as we search within our own thinking. We can keep so busy taking the mites out of our brother's eyes that we have no time to work on the beam in our own vision, paraphrasing what Jesus the Christ said.

All of my wonderful teachers in the past several years have been unaware that they were helping me. They were simply being their infuriating selves.

How To Help And Teach

Instead of sharing spiritual principles when we see people in need, we simply put these principles into action in our own lives. If someone asks for help directly, that is another matter. If you are to help someone, they will ask. If in doubt about whether to help or not, wait until you are sure you are being asked. If you are not sure you are being asked . . . you are **not** being asked. This applies to individual treatments, group healings, giving advice, or sharing insights.   It applies to any intervention.

When you are sure you have been asked and are being directed by guidance to be involved, the rest is easy. You simply go within and **"listen"** and you will be told what to do.

But what happens if someone needs help, continues to violate the principles we know are true, but does not ask?   For me it works like this. Another person is upset or in trouble and that bothers me.   I feel upset since I see them in need (a false perception). Feeling out of peace is a **signal** that I need to turn within for guidance for myself.   I don't try to fix their problem, but I **"accept"** that I see a problem. Since I'm upset or see a need, I must have a false perception. I remember I have a choice to see them as having a problem (which is what appears to be real) or to see them as my loving friend come to bless me (which does not appear to be the case).

105

I choose to see the loving friend and ask inner guidance for help to get beyond the appearance to the real truth. I ask, "What is my blessing here?" What then? I am still and **"listen"** and **"accept"** what is happening. As I wait, if thoughts occur which are not peaceful, I turn within again and ask for clarity and peace. I may have to continue this practice over a long period of time, or peace may come right away.

Each time I do not feel loving and peaceful toward another, each time I do not experience someone as perfect and whole without any problems, I begin the process again of **"accepting"** the truth. I am patient, knowing who is in charge and what the outcome will be. It will be perfect. I will ultimately see that we are both perfect and all is well.

As I **"listen"** within, I may hear many things. Here are some examples of what I've heard on such occasions:

"What the other person is doing is perfect; don't be deceived by appearances."

"Do not withdraw your love simply because it does not appear to be returned."

"Each time you are tempted by a seeming lack of love, remember all the other person's wonderful qualities and be grateful."

"Let them continue to be angry and make no response."

"Let them know you are upset and share how you feel without holding them responsible."

"They cannot hurt you and you cannot hurt them."

At one time or another when I have been upset and hurt, I have heard one or more such messages.

106

If you do as suggested, you will hear what is perfect for you in each occasion, and then you have only to do it. When I acted in accordance with what I heard, I always found peace.

The Proof That It's Working

After **"listening"** and **"accepting"** and following the guidance, the proof that it is working is we feel more love and gratitude toward everything, including the other people and ourselves. We cannot verify the results if we look outside ourselves for the evidence. We cannot look for the other people to change as confirmation of our healing. They will seldom change their actions, especially in a short time, but their effect on us will change immediately. Their actions will no longer bother us. We will be able to think of them and feel only love for them. We know they are doing what they need to do. We will not desire to change them in any way. The healing has occurred when **you can never experience them in the old way again.**

This does not mean we need to stay near them or avoid them. They simply will not bother us. When they are near, we check inside and see that we are more peaceful. We may not feel totally peaceful at first, but we will have moved in that direction. In time we will have total peace and feel love for them. We may be led by inner guidance to stay near them or leave, but never as a way to avoid our discomfort. These adjustments will happen naturally as the healing is occurring without our efforts.

In cases of physical abuse or at those times when the situation is so challenging that we cannot be peaceful enough to do our inner work, a move or short absence may be necessary to achieve a temporary respite. The real healing will only occur, however, when we change our thinking about ourselves and **"accept"** the other person as he or she is.

Leaving a situation will never heal it. This is because the need for healing is only in our minds. As has often been said, "No matter where you go, there you are." You cannot run away from your mind or change what it thinks by changing locations.

A temporary distancing or a temporary respite from fear or pain is sometimes helpful. This action falls in the same category of expediency as making a plan, keeping a list or setting a goal. It is not wrong to do things that help us get our peace and reduce our fears. We are only asked to do the best we can. If it is necessary to do something such as move away or avoid contact to reduce fear, do it. It is **never** helpful to continue things that bring up great fear. This is not a process of proving our toughness. Recognize, however, that this temporary change will not bring a healing of the situation and that you will face a similar situation again and again until your thinking changes. Always be willing to turn to inner guidance and ask what to do. You will be led clearly to stay or go, to be still or answer, or given some other direction. **"Listening"** is the only real answer in every situation. Now let's look at the issue of control and how **"acceptance"** helps us move past this blockage to inner guidance.

Chapter 8

"ACCEPTANCE" THE OPPOSITE OF CONTROL

"Accepting" Frees Us From The Control Prison

A major issue for most of us is control. We fear that if we do not control every situation, we will be hurt. Most of our training in life is designed to increase our ability to control. Control is our favorite method of finding safety in this world. Our fears, caused by a belief that we are surrounded by dangerous conditions, dictate our defensive actions. Fear takes many forms, from direct attacks, to resistance toward what we dislike.

We can control by seeking to make another guilty and ourselves right. These passive/aggressive actions often seem less harmful, but they are still a form of attack. Control can be given many names that do not appear to be negative, such as education and improvement, justice and repayment, or just doing what is "expected" and "right." The form is not important, nor is the name used to describe the action. What is important is the intent of the perpetrator.

We Control In Many Ways

Isn't it important for you to know something about others before you are "comfortable"? Can you imagine feeling good about always being out of control? Do you avoid certain people and places to feel more comfortable? OK, we agree, we all like to feel in control.

This desire to control each situation is part of our survival instinct. It can cause us to make some very bad decisions and to avoid things which have come to bless us. It is founded on the belief that we are residents of a hostile world and need to always be alert for possible danger or attack.

Four Steps That Release Control

We don't need to squelch these control desires, but we can begin to move beyond them by not acting on them and seeing them as limitations.

Step One: We need to be aware of our true feelings which are fearful and manifest, on occasions, as the desire to control and change others. We must be willing to see what our desires are. We should not cover up these desires by thinking they are natural and right. If we miss this step, we only bury our fears deeper.

Denial of our feelings of fear is not effective in removing our fears, it only temporarily covers them up. The ostrich approach of putting our heads in the sand does not work. The feelings and the fears will surface again and again until we look at them and move past them. Each new time we are faced with a fear, it will appear larger and more threatening. So the sooner we face these fears the better it is. We do not have to dig them out, that is not necessary. We do have to recognize them as they surface, and acknowledge them as **our** fears in order to have a healing.

Step Two: We ask for assistance from our inner guide. The central idea is to be quiet and then move beyond our fearful mind. We do this by releasing all thought of what needs to be done, and going past the fear to a quiet place of openness. It is helpful to become disinterested observers of the event and thereby reduce our emotions. As we become more quiet, thoughts will occur to us. We simply observe them as we would a movie and then we let them go as the plot continues. I find it helpful to watch my thoughts as if I were reading a ticker tape or a moving billboard. We will know we are in a receptive state when we feel, even for a short time, peaceful and open to a new outlook. At this point the movie is usually over, at least it's intermission.

Step Three: We "**accept**" what appears to be. This moves us straight toward and eventually past the fear. We release, even if only for a moment, the desire to change the situation.   We consider the possibility that the situation is coming for our benefit, even if it appears harmful or distasteful.   If possible we seek to be grateful for some aspect of the situation. We release the idea that we know what is going on. We are looking for inspiration. This is not thinking or understanding; it is seeing with new eyes, a new perspective.

Step Four: We wait until we hear guidance. How do we know it is guidance? If you ask that question, you probably are not getting guidance. You will know when you are guided because you will see things anew. You will say, "*Of course!*" You will have a feeling of certainty and peace.

Wanting the final outcome to be clear before you take the next step is another form of trying to stay in control. When we think about the long-range results, we usually create additional fear. Finally, if we **"listen"** we will feel calm and clear about the next step.

I asked my inner guide once, why guidance always came step-by-step. "*Wouldn't it be possible to tell me several days in advance what will be happening? I know it would make me feel safer sometimes,"* I said. He replied, *"Lee, I'd like to tell you sooner. But if I did, you'd just try to help it along. Frankly, I don't need your help. It would just delay things."* I'm sure he's quite right. I do like to help even when I don't know how.

Now the most important thing of all -- when we do know we are guided, we must ACT on what we hear. We must take the next step. Only then will we get results. For example, we hear to wait, to do nothing about the situation. Then what we must do is wait, not seek to hurry things along or run around searching for new solutions.

Is Control Effective?

Let's take an honest look at this desire to control. Have you really been effective in your control of past situations or other people? If you have not been successful in the past, why do you think continued efforts will be successful? When you tried to control, was your judgment of the situation and what needed to be done correct? I don't mean just correct for you, but for everyone. Haven't many things you resisted at the outset become helpful? Maybe even joyful? Have not many lost opportunities turned out to be blessings in disguise. How often have you changed your mind about things? If you could totally control the situation, would you really know what was best for all concerned? Are not many of your desires for outcomes in conflict? Do you even **know** what is best for you?

Next time the desire to control occurs to you, look at it honestly and consider all the consequences, then ask yourself if you still want to control. Be aware of the fact that much of our desire to control is an attempt to achieve a **fantasy**. The reality of the situation is often quite different from our fantasy which never existed and could never happen.

Looked at clearly, the desire to control loses much of its appeal and can often be suspended. This suspension is all that is required to begin to "**accept**" things as they are. We do not have to like things in order to "**accept**" them. We merely need to doubt that we have a better solution. Now with an open mind, we can begin to observe what is really going on and remain peaceful. Even in stressful situations, we can suspend the desire to control for just a moment, so we can "**accept**" and "**listen**". The reality is that each situation is a potential **blessing**.

Standing On The Edge Of Uncertainty

"**Accepting**" what is, we may not know what to do, nor need we try to figure anything out. We stand on the edge of uncertainty, confident that we have a source available which is certain. This inner wisdom and strength will step forward as we step back and loosen our tight grip on the safety line of control. This is not a real safety line, but the shackles of control. Our freedom is embodied in Jesus the Christ's words, *"Not my will but Thine be done."*

Control is the desire beneath the idea, *"I do not like this and wish it were different."* While this may seem too general a statement, I have found it always true in my life. Letting go of my desire to have things, places, or people, including myself, be different, opens my mind to a new perspective.

This Is The Essence Of "Accepting."

This ability to experience everything as perfect is not just knowing or trusting that things will be all right. It is the actual experience in daily living that nothing exists but God, the Divine, and His Perfection is everywhere here and now. We have the vision to see that no change, correction, or lesson is necessary. What is needed is here and being done. Now we are willing and eager to let go of control, so we can see what is really happening. It is a most exciting and joyful experience. Everything is new and wonderful, coming to us as **blessings** beyond measure. Who would want to change that?

This World Doesn't Work

Why doesn't the world seem to work until we **"accept?"** I believe there are four reasons.

First, we look at the world only from our own perspective which does not include all other people and things. This gives us a limited, distorted viewpoint regarding people and events, and one not consistent with God's Reality which sees all things as connected.

Second, we don't see all aspects or dimensions of what we observe. Mostly we miss the spiritual aspect which is the central overriding one. So we are very concerned with the form of things and seldom aware of the content. In short, we see the outside but miss the essence of what is happening. We are programed to see only the material and physical and not the spiritual content of things.

Third, we don't know who we are. We do not realize we are spiritual beings. We see ourselves only as physical and material and judge all things as they affect this concept. Thus we direct attention to our physical and temporal needs and place little emphasis on the eternal and spiritual sustenance. Since we are truly a spiritual being, we will never be satisfied with the human, the material, and the limited. Being never satisfied with this world and its conditions is not our failure, but a positive step in the direction of our spiritual Reality.

Fourth, we are very concerned with time, mostly the future and the past. We judge all things based on our past experiences as we remember them. We approach the future in relation to these past remembrances which are never totally accurate. This makes us repeat faulty concepts and reject everything that conflicts with our perceptions.

The world doesn't work because of our perspective and perceptions. We apply a faulty measurement and therefore obtain faulty results. The world is not a solid thing but molds to our viewpoints. In our present state, our viewpoints are limited. The only change needed is that of viewpoint.

The Chart

I was given a visual demonstration of this by my inner guide. He pointed out that all maps and charts are drawn from a higher perspective than what the eye sees at ground level. A chart shows the land and sea as it would be seen from an airplane.

My inner guide reminded me of my experience as a sailor. From sea level, a group of islands and rocks often seems to be a solid mass of land. The channels of water between the islands are not always visible to the pilot of a boat. When the pilot looks at the charts, he can see clearly where the channels are and how to navigate between the land and rocks in safety.

"**Listening**" is like looking at a chart. It gives us a higher perspective. It shows clearly where to go when there seems to be blockage and danger. The pilot, by use of his charts, "**accepts**" that there is a clear passage even when it appears there is no safe way to proceed. By relying on his charts, which give him a different, higher perspective, the experienced pilot brings his craft into a safe harbor.

"**Listening**" does the same for all who use it. It does not really change anything, it simply brings a higher perspective (clarity, wisdom, and vision) to the situation. Using it, we can safely go where there appears to be blockage and danger.

The Spiritual Trip

"Spiritual" is not always what we think it is. Often it is the opposite of what I think it should be. This truth was brought home during an early speaking tour I took through the Northwest. It was one of the first efforts I made to share what I was learning. I still had a small advertising business which supported me, but I was able to travel and lecture part of the year, if the contributions paid my travel expenses.

I was proud of the fact that I was sustained on these trips by donations. It felt very spiritual. I was aware of the spiritual truth that God was my supply and I thought I knew how that supply should manifest.

For much of the trip, I got nice donations but they were only enough to cover my expenses until I arrived at the Unity Church in Tacoma. There I presented a day-long workshop and at the end I was given, for me at the time, a very large donation (about $700).

That night camping in my van, I thought, *"If I could get a donation like this each week, I could just lecture and give up the advertising business."* That possibility thrilled me for several days and I thought my direction was becoming clear.

I arrived in Seattle and gave a small evening lecture at a center operated by friends. It was not until everyone left that I realized no one had mentioned giving a donation to me. The little donation basket was sitting by the door, empty. I felt something was wrong but shrugged it off. *"Oh well, God is my supply,"* I thought, and went to my car.

I did not feel good about what had happened. I tried to think thoughts that would make my upset go away. Instead, an inner argument occurred. *"It is not the money that makes me mad."* I thought, *"It's the idea that no one cared enough to offer a donation. Oh well, I am staying free with my brother, so it's all right. No it's not. Even a penny would have felt better. I feel like I'm not appreciated. Oh well, look at the donation I got in Tacoma. It all evens out. No it doesn't. I do not like what happened."* This went on for quite a while, but I got no resolution. Finally I asked my inner guide what this was all about. I was getting more and more upset. That's always a sure sign I need to **"listen."** Something I usually put off until all else fails.

My inner guide said, "*What do you expect when you don't ask?*" I gave him lots of excuses about why I did not ask. I said, "*I didn't ask because it isn't spiritual to have needs.*" I said, "*The chairman of the meeting should be the one to ask.*"

My inner guide said, "*Those are not the real reasons you don't ask. You don't ask because you don't want to be dependent on or obligated to others. You never have.*" I knew it was true. (It's really hard to fool your inner guide.) I always loved to give, but had a very hard time receiving. I didn't like feeling obligated.

I saw it was a pattern that had affected my whole life. I didn't want to be indebted to anyone, it made me feel less than whole. If I had to accept something, even a compliment, I would always try to repay it quickly with a greater one. I did not like to accept gifts, especially since there might be strings attached. I saw my giving was often coupled with a desire to be superior. I had thought my generosity was good, but saw it now as also a desire to be separate and apart. It was a protection that I needed to be safe.

My strong desire to give was being used by my inner guidance to get me to share what I was learning about "**listening**." That is another observation I have made; both my "good" and "bad" qualities are used by my spiritual guide. He has told me he can use anything. Most of the time I experience him using what I call "bad" qualities. I am sure for a great deal of my life, he used my sex drive to guide me. Now, my inner guide was using my compulsive desire **to give** to get me to share about "**listening**."

"What can I do about this?" I asked my guide. I heard, *"Each time you give a workshop or lecture you are to be the one to ask for a donation. Do not pass this job to someone else. "You are to say to everyone present, 'I know my source of supply is God, but it manifests through you. If I am to continue to travel and lecture, I need your support. Please give what you wish and know it is greatly appreciated.'"* I said something like this at my lectures for over a year. It was very hard to do. Many groups who sponsored me were glad to be relieved of the responsibility of asking for a donation. Some people even changed their minds about asking for donations and charging for their work after hearing this story. I am one. Now I always charge what I am guided to charge.

Giving and Recieving

My inner guide constantly reminded me during this time that one of my greatest joys was to give. He said, *"When you do not receive, you do not give another the chance to feel the joy of giving."* Shortly after the incident in Seattle, I was given another piece of the "Giving and Receiving" puzzle.

A young man in Oregon requested a private consultation. He asked before we started, how much I charged and mentioned he did not have much money. I assured him we would find a way to decide what would be right for all concerned. During the consultation it became evident that the major issue was supply. I don't remember all that was said, but I know by the end of the session I was convinced he recognized his infinite supply. Then he asked me how much he owed. I told him my inner guide had instructed that we both meditate on how much money should change hands. We were to be quiet and open our minds to infinite supply and realize that giving and receiving were the same. Maybe he was to give me something or maybe I was to give something to him. We would ask and then do what we heard. He agreed that sounded like a great idea.

We closed our eyes for a time and when we opened them I asked if he had heard to do anything. I had heard nothing except to continue to support the idea of infinite supply. He said, *"Yes,"* and opened his wallet. He gave me all he had, a ten dollar bill. I caught my breath and almost said, *"No that's too much. Don't give all you have."* My guide reminded me to be quiet and remember supply is infinite. I took his last ten dollars, knowing we had both been healed in a wonderful way.

My part was to receive and know that it did not impoverish him in any way. By taking the money, I demonstrated I knew our supply was infinite. By giving, he demonstrated he knew the same truth. It was not easy in this case to receive. In fact, it would have been much easier to give him money. That, however, would have been an acknowledgement of his neediness and not a demonstration of my faith in our abundance.

The point of these two stories is that we don't know what is really happening spiritually most of the time.

This material human world will not work. Thank God we cannot make it work through our efforts. Only by **"accepting"** can we see that everything is perfect.

Chapter 9

IN CONCLUSION

What is most evident in the whole process of change is Oneness. I see others coming into my awareness at the right time and leaving at the right time. That timing is not based on my desires, but on everyone's real needs. We are never really separate or apart from each other or our Source, except in physical appearance. I am beginning to glimpse and trust that Reality. As I do, I experience the connection that we all share.

I have learned not to hold another to me or have them leave based on my perceived needs. I am willing for the process of change to occur and participate with no sadness, but only love and **"acceptance."** I am beginning to lessen the distance between my self called **"me"** and my other self called **"them."** My next process, **"being"**, which started last year, is to lessen the distance between my self called **"me"** and my other self called **"Christ."**

"BEING"

As I finish this book, I can report I have tried the process of **"being"** in the latter part of 1990 and in early 1991. At present I have no idea what will occur next. I have been asked to *"give no thought"* as to where I will live, how I will be fed, or what I should do.

"Being" is a most challenging process. I am not asked to not have needs. I am asked to give *"no thought"* to fulfilling those needs through my own efforts. My normal reaction is to worry about and plan for my future. The majority of my thoughts, in the past, have been about filling my needs. This is wasted effort. I could better spend the time enjoying what is now and being aware of all the joy and happiness that is available. How often do I lose joy by *"giving thought"*? Can I claim my birthright as a spiritual being, now? I know in my heart the answer is *"yes,"* but do I have the courage to act only on that answer?

The Three Processes Are Really One

"Accepting" is complete and **"being"** has started. When it's done I will share it with you. These three, **"listening,"** **"accepting,"** and **"being,"** are really one concept, **"Oneness"**. They appear different to aid in my awareness of them. The conclusion of all awareness is **"Oneness."** I enjoy sharing my processes with you because in doing so they become clearer to me. I leave you with this thought regarding **"Oneness"**.

Oneness:

There is One Mind, One Life, One Truth, One Love. All is part of One Creation; all is connected and all is alike. Only total integrity and total communication exist in God's Reality and this is expressed as Love, Truth, and Life, with no opposite. Perceived separation is our only problem. Connection with our Source is the only path. We turn within and **"listen"** to realize this connection. We **"accept"** all that comes to us. It is only Love and that is all we can **"be"**.

Until we meet again I honor your commitment to spiritual awareness because your efforts are made on everyone's behalf.

GOD BLESS.

GLOSSARY

GOD - When I say "God", I mean the unchanging, loving, beautiful, joyful source of all life and being. This Source manifests as eternal principles which apply in all circumstances, both spiritual and material. God is not the name of the Divine Source, since It cannot be encompassed with limited ideas and words. I often use the pronoun "He" in place of the word "God," but of course God is not male or female but includes all attributes. Since He created male and female in His likeness it is obvious that both genders are included equally. I could use the pronoun "it" but I do not experience God as impersonal, which that word implies. To use the term He/She creates an idea of conflict, a combination which raises more issues than necessary. These issues are very human in nature and have nothing to do with the Divine. The terms "God" and "He" are short, traditional words which have general acceptance and therefore I find them most useful. I have capitalized all words, terms, or concepts which I have used to describe Deity. The idea of an unlimited Source cannot be contained in a name or gender or concept since these ideas are attempts to define and limit things. We, as humans, think in limited concepts and we need these concepts at present to communicate ideas. Therefore I have chosen these words to communicate that which is not capable of total communication by using words.

GOD'S LAWS - These are the only principles which are always in operation everywhere and cannot be broken or avoided. They govern the way creation interrelates. They seem to be absent when we ignore them, but they always determine what is. There is no punishment for the breaking of these laws since they are incapable of being broken. They can be compared to the law of gravity. Its effect here on earth is always operational. If you step off a cliff you will fall. If you use a hang glider, you will appear to avoid the law of gravity but you will eventually come back to the ground. You are not punished for trying to avoid the law of gravity. If we are to fly successfully, we must be aware of the law of gravity. God's laws operate in this same way. They are always present and always active. To be happy, we must be aware of them.

SPIRITUAL - When I speak of spiritual, I mean what is eternal and unseen. Love, Truth, and Life are some attributes of the unseen spiritual Reality of which we are aware. Beauty, joy, laughter, tenderness, and compassion are evidence of this unseen power. As you will find in this book anger, hate, lack, and pain are also evidence of the spiritual principle in operation. They are not powers but signals. Their presence gives warning that we are losing our awareness of our spiritual source and seeking to violate Reality's laws. What is spiritual is eternal, unchanging, and always produces the same results in all circumstances. What is spiritual is "Reality", as I use that term. Reality never changes. Reality is all that is. It is the only existence.

MATERIAL - What is material is temporary and always changing. That is always the test. If something will change, it is material, not spiritual. Material is neither good nor bad, it is fluid and illusory. It should be recognized as such and not depended upon. Material laws are not really laws but beliefs. They represent the concepts of their maker, each one of us. We need to recognize that no beliefs are universally agreed upon. We all have different beliefs, concepts, and perceptions. What is beauty or truth to one observer is not always beauty or truth to another. Since what is material is seen, this means we do not all see in the same way. Material is not reality but duality. It may at anytime represent one of two or more concepts. Materiality will be good or bad depending on whether it matches the concepts of the perceiver. What is good to one may be bad to another. Time is just one of our material concepts. Your inner guide can use and change material concepts or "laws" to assist in your spiritual awareness.

CHRIST - By the word "Christ," I mean the Son of God or Creation of God. The Creation or Son of the unlimited was made in His likeness and is also unlimited because His Source is Divine. The term "Christ" describes in a traditional way the concept of a spiritually created or Divine Being. The Divine has infinite expression both in Reality and in the material world. There have been many who have expressed the concept of Christ in their lives. Some more fully than others. Some never used the term "Christ" yet expressed the concept in an outstanding way. Like Its Creator the Christ is neither male or female but embodies all qualities of the Divine in full measure.

JESUS - Jesus, as I think of him, was a man who embodied the concept of the Christ in his life so well that he became synonymous with the term. He demonstrated he was a spiritual Being through teaching, healing, and compassion. For me, Jesus demonstrated perfectly how to live a spiritual life. He gave proof that we are all "the Sons of God." I know many of you have created images of Christ in your mind which relate to suffering, sacrifice, and guilt. I also realize that some of you do not accept the idea of Jesus as the Christ. Jesus is not the only example of Sonship with the Divine. You may have chosen other examples which you feel work for you and that is fine. Whatever form of Divine Connection helps you accept your divinity is the one for you to use. For me, Jesus is a wonderful source of inner guidance and a beautiful example of how to live my life. So I may from time to time share how this concept has been meaningful to me. I do not intend to suggest that my form of accepting Divinity is superior or that you should adopt it. On the contrary, I propose you use the forms that appeal to you and not get all hung up on words and images. It is the basic idea that is important, not the labels.

PERFECTION (REALITY) - Perfection is what is. It is the only Reality. It is God's Reality. Perfect is not the result of comparison against a preconceived standard. That idea of "perfection" is simply a form of human judgment. Since judgment is always changing so the human standard of "perfection" is always changing. Real perfection sees all of creation as being in harmony. No tree or flower or landscape is more perfect or more beautiful than another. Each expresses itself perfectly and blends into a perfect picture whether it be seascape, desert, mountain, or forest glen. True perfection does not compare. It celebrates all that is. In every way this perfect "beingness" nurtures and pleases us. Perfection is the truth of creation and the beauty behind all forms. We start our processes of awareness of perfection by turning to the Divine connection. God is perfection's source. God's creation is perfection's expression. As a part of creation, we are all perfect.

INNER GUIDE   OR INNER GUIDANCE - This is the inner voice I talk about in both this book and "Listening." In the Bible, it would be the angels who ministered to the prophets or the Holy Ghost who came to comfort the disciples.   It is the "still small voice." It is always with us though we can try to deny it. It comes in many, many forms and will appear to you in the form you most easily accept. It requires only our willingness and stillness to be heard. It is guiding and caring for us even when we are unaware. Awareness of our inner guide's presence brings clarity and peace. It is our ever present connection to our Divine Source. This cannot be broken by anything or any event at any time. We can, however, decide to avoid listening to it. It is not capitalized in this book because it is the link between or a combination of the Divine and the human or material.

ACCEPTING - This is the act of allowing what is, to be. Accepting is not giving our approval to what we do not like, nor does it require our understanding something. It is an act of non-judgment and forgiveness. Like "listening," "accepting" is consciousness and awareness. Its purpose is to reveal what is really happening and to dissolve what we think is happening when that is not real. We can see Reality only by releasing our false beliefs and concepts. Behind the facade of conflict and pain, we will always find perfection. Like the lifting of the fog, "accepting" reveals what always was there but was unseen. It does not bring change but a feeling of clarity and release. It needs to be coupled with a willingness to "listen" and frees us from the necessity of seeking changes outside ourselves. No real changes ever occur outside our minds.

TEN ATTITUDES OF "ACCEPTANCE"

1. If I am disturbed, I do not understand what is happening. I am willing to open my mind to all possibilities and "listen" for clarity. I do this without a desire to change anything.

2. What I don't like in my life or in the world is caused by my false beliefs about myself. These false beliefs are really limitations, but may feel like protection. They are not caused by others or their actions, despite believable appearances to the contrary.

3. When others do things that bother me, I have the choice to use that upset to uncover false beliefs I hold about myself. The "button" they push that disturbs me is the key to my clarity and the door to my freedom from limitation.

4. I can therefore be grateful for this revelation, even though it is unpleasant to have my "buttons" pushed. The "button" is directly connected to a false belief I hold about myself. As I see this falsity and release the belief, I gain freedom and expand my ability to be happy.

5. I cannot fix others or myself through my own efforts or by using my mind, since it is my mind which is causing the problem. I merely need to change my mind about the situation or person to change the effects. This change is brought about by asking my inner guide for assistance and releasing my own judgment.

6. My understanding is never necessary for me to love. I need only to honor and respect others not understand them. When I do this I also learn to honor and respect myself.

7. I really have no power in my present state to control things in this world. My attempts to control are merely fantasies. Love is in control of everything therefore there is no need to control.

8. I am willing, even if only for a moment, to give up my concepts of what is happening and my desire to control or change things and become a neutral observer of each distress in which I think I am involved. If I am still for a moment and truly "listen", God will lead the way.

9. I do not know what is "good" or "bad" for me or for others. I see I have often been wrong in the past when I tried to judge what was "right" or "good". I am willing to give up my judgment of all appearances. I have an inner source which does know and will guide me. As I release judgment I will see the Truth.

10. No matter what I see or think, God's laws are in action. All other appearances are false in this world. I can place myself under the laws of Grace by letting go of my false perceptions, ideas, and concepts.

Lee Coit 1991

For information:
Las Brisas Publishing, P.O. Box 500, Wildomar, CA 92595

TEN ATTITUDES OF "ACCEPTANCE"

1. If I am disturbed, I do not understand what is happening. I am willing to open my mind to all possibilities and "listen" for clarity. I do this without a desire to change anything.

2. What I don't like in my life or in the world is caused by my false beliefs about myself. These false beliefs are really limitations, but may feel like protection. They are not caused by others or their actions, despite believable appearances to the contrary.

3. When others do things that bother me, I have the choice to use that upset to uncover false beliefs I hold about myself. The "button" they push that disturbs me is the key to my clarity and the door to my freedom from limitation.

4. I can therefore be grateful for this revelation, even though it is unpleasant to have my "buttons" pushed. The "button" is directly connected to a false belief I hold about myself. As I see this falsity and release the belief, I gain freedom and expand my ability to be happy.

5. I cannot fix others or myself through my own efforts or by using my mind, since it is my mind which is causing the problem. I merely need to change my mind about the situation or person to change the effects. This change is brought about by asking my inner guide for assistance and releasing my own judgment.

6. My understanding is never necessary for me to love. I need only to honor and respect others not understand them. When I do this I also learn to honor and respect myself.

7. I really have no power in my present state to control things in this world. My attempts to control are merely fantasies. Love is in control of everything therefore there is no need to control.

8. I am willing, even if only for a moment, to give up my concepts of what is happening and my desire to control or change things and become a neutral observer of each distress in which I think I am involved. If I am still for a moment and truly "listen", God will lead the way.

9. I do not know what is "good" or "bad" for me or for others. I see I have often been wrong in the past when I tried to judge what was "right" or "good". I am willing to give up my judgment of all appearances. I have an inner source which does know and will guide me. As I release judgment I will see the Truth.

10. No matter what I see or think, God's laws are in action. All other appearances are false in this world. I can place myself under the laws of Grace by letting go of my false perceptions, ideas, and concepts.

Lee Coit 1991

For information:
Las Brisas Publishing, P.O. Box 500, Wildomar, CA 92595

LECTURE AND WORKSHOP INFORMATION

Lee Coit has committed his life to following his inner voice in all things. For many years he has traveled and lectured worldwide helping others increase their awareness of their inner guide. He is available for lectures and seminars anywhere and makes every effort to respond to all requests.

If you would like to attend a workshop please send us your name. We will then notify you of the time and place when we are coming to your area. If you want to sponsor such an event please let us know. Sponsorship is quite easy. When we have enough interest for several workshops in one part of the world we plan a trip to that area. We only ask that each group guarantee ten people. Of course, we will offer lectures and workshops for any size group. The workshop can be held in a home or a public facility. We are primarily interested in the desire of the attendees to increase their spiritual awareness, we are not concerned with numbers, revenues, or exposure.

The cost of our workshops at this time is about $50.00 per day per person for a 5 hour session. We offer either one or two day sessions and are open to longer workshops if there is a desire. If we are requested to make a special trip to an area we ask that our travel expenses be covered in addition to the workshop fees. Please write for our complete brochure regarding sponsoring an event if you are interested. We are happy to discuss the matter with you. WE WOULD LOVE TO COME TO YOUR AREA SOMETIME AND SHARE THIS WONDERFUL PROCESS WITH YOU AND YOUR FRIENDS.

YOUR FAVORITE BOOK STORE SHOULD HAVE OUR MATERIAL. IF NOT THEY CAN ORDER IT FROM MOST MAJOR DISTRIBUTORS.

However if you prefer to use mail order we have books and tapes available which deal with the many facets of "Listening." These are the items available as of December 1, 1991. Please write for our current catalog as new items are added yearly.

BOOKS:

LISTENING - How to Increase Awareness of Your Inner Guide, by Lee Coit

This has become the classic guide book for anyone seeking to connect with their Spiritual Source.　It is now also available overseas in several foreign languages. Published first in 1985, it is 96 pages of practical suggestions and tips regarding inner guidance.

Price is $6.95 plus $1.50 postage and handling. Include sales tax if California resident.

LISTENING... STILL - How to Increase Your Awareness of Perfection, by Lee Coit

This book broadens the concept of "Listening." It explains the process of "Accepting" which takes "Listening" to another level. It discusses the discovery of "Listening" and how the author uses these two processes in his life. Published in 1991, it is 144 pages of insights and information about applying spiritual principles in your life.

Price is $8.95　plus $1.50 postage and handling. Include sales tax if California resident.

TAPES:

LISTENING I - "An Introduction"

A ninety minute tape which includes two live 45 minute lectures introducing the concept of "Listening." One side uses everyday language and would be understood by anyone of any background. The second side explains the concepts in more spiritual terms. The material is presented without script or preparation so that you experience inner guidance as Lee Coit hears it.

LISTENING II - "A 90 Minute Workshop"

This is a live workshop with audience participation and questions. You will feel the joy and excitement of Lee Coit's inner guided seminars. As with all tapes there is no script or other preparation. What occurs is inner directed and spontaneous.

The price of each tape is $10.95 plus $1.50 postage and handling.

Include sales tax if California Resident.

BE THIN FOREVER - Inner Listening to achieve and maintain your ideal weight by Vikki Coit.

A 60 minute lecture in which Vikki tells how she overcame overeating without diet and deprivation by using inner "listening." This tape has changed thousands of lives.

The price is $9.95 plus $1.50 for postage and handling.

Include sales tax if California resident.

LOVING RELATIONSHIPS WITHOUT COMPROMISE
Lee and Vikki Coit share the secrets of having great relationships with everyone especially those close to you. This live sixty minute lecture discusses how to be loving without sacrificing yourself.

The price is $9.95 plus $1.50 for postage and handling.

Include sales tax if California resident.

ANY COMBINATION OF TEN (10) ITEMS EARNS A QUANTITY DISCOUNT OF THIRTY PERCENT (30%) OFF THE TOTAL UNIT PRICE. PLEASE ADD $6.00 FOR POSTAGE AND HANDLING PER EACH 10 ITEMS ORDER. PLEASE INCLUDE THE TAX IF CALIFORNIA RESIDENT.

Send your check with your order to:
Las Brisas Publishing
PO Box 500
Wildomar, CA 92595